By the same author

Carrying the Fire: An Astronaut's Journeys (1974)

Liftoff: The Story of America's Adventure in Space (1988)

Mission to Mars (1990)

FLYING TO THE MOON

THE MOON

AN ASTRONAUT'S STORY

FLYING TO

MICHAEL COLLINS

THE **MOON**

AN ASTRONAUT'S STORY

*Fully revised and updated edition for the 50th anniversary
of Apollo 11, the first manned lunar landing*

Introduction by **Captain Scott Kelly,**
former commander of the International Space Station

FARRAR STRAUS GIROUX | NEW YORK

Photographs following page 48 are from the collection of the author, unless otherwise noted. Photographs following page 176 are from NASA's Apollo 11 image archives.

Farrar Straus Giroux Books for Young Readers
An imprint of Macmillan Children's Publishing Group, LLC
175 Fifth Avenue, New York, NY 10010

1 3 5 7 9 10 8 6 4 2

mackids.com

Library of Congress Cataloging-in-Publication Data
Collins, Michael.
Flying to the moon : an astronaut's story / Michael Collins.
3rd ed., with a pref. and a rev. final chapter.
p. cm.
ISBN: 978-0-374-42356-8 (pbk.)
1. Collins, Michael.—Juvenile literature. 2. Space flight to the moon—Juvenile literature. [1. Collins, Michael. 2. Astronauts. 3. Space flight to the moon.] I. Collins, Michael. Carrying the fire. II. Title.
TL789.85.C65 A3 1994 629.45/0092—dc20 [B] 93-42001 CIP AC
Revised edition ISBN: 978-0-374-31202-2

Our books may be purchased in bulk for promotional, educational, or business use. Please contact your local bookseller or the Macmillan Corporate and Premium Sales Department at (800) 221-7945 ext. 5442 or by email at MacmillanSpecialMarkets@macmillan.com.

This book is based in part on *Carrying the Fire*, copyright © 1974 by Michael Collins

To Kate and Ann

INTRODUCTION

Captain Scott Kelly

One of my earliest memories is from the summer when I was five, a night when my parents woke my twin brother and me from a deep sleep and carried us out into the living room. We settled on the rug and looked up at the TV, where a blurry shape was bounding around in black and white. Our parents explained that a man named Neil Armstrong was, right at that moment, walking on the surface of the Moon. We sat glued to the screen as Neil Armstrong and Buzz Aldrin planted an American flag on the Moon's surface and saluted. The newscaster explained that while the two men were carrying out their tasks on the surface, a third member of the crew was orbiting the Moon above them. Michael Collins, the command module pilot, was alone in the spacecraft that would carry the three astronauts back to Earth. I didn't understand the CMP's role any more than I understood the concept of men walking on the surface of another planetary body—it seemed that the Moon we were talking about couldn't possibly be the same Moon that hung outside my bedroom window at night.

Some thirty-five years after that exciting night, I was seated next to Michael Collins at an Astronaut Reunion Dinner, an event held every other year that brings together active and retired astronauts from across generations. He greeted me warmly, and I told him I was excited to get to meet him. When I addressed him as General Collins, he corrected me: "I'm just ol' Mike."

Mike seemed much younger than his years—talking with him was more like talking with someone my own age rather than a retired hero decades older. He was bright and alert, with all the details of his experiences still at his fingertips, and always ready with a self-effacing joke. I instantly liked him.

When I asked Mike about Apollo 11 and what he remembered, he said he had spent some time thinking about what would happen if Neil and Buzz found themselves unable to lift off the surface of the Moon—a distinct possibility because the lunar module had never been fully tested. Mike knew that if he returned home from the Moon alone, that would be his legacy—he would spend the rest of his life as the man who came back without his crewmates. He also told me he had no regrets about not walking on the Moon himself. He understood the importance of his role, and he was proud to have gotten to carry it out.

Later, I had the chance to reflect on the role Mike played in the Apollo 11 crew. Neil Armstrong was famously introverted—he preferred to avoid the spotlight and eventually stopped appearing in public, with rare exceptions, until his death in 2012—and Buzz Aldrin is quite the opposite, seeking out opportunities to talk about his adventures in space and the future of spaceflight whenever he can. Mike was the perfect balancing point between the two of them: more affable and outgoing than Armstrong, but humbler and more retiring than Aldrin. He never walked on the Moon (he would certainly have had the chance to do so on a later mission, but he stepped aside to let others have the chance), and no postage stamps bear the image of his face. But Mike's role in our nation's finest moment was as crucial as Neil's or Buzz's, and without him piloting the command module, the Moon landing never would have happened. He held the historic Apollo 11 mission together in more ways than one.

My generation was changed by watching the accomplishments of Apollo 11—not only by the technological advances the Moon landings helped bring about, but also by the pride the entire nation took in the daring and accomplishments of those three men. For my parents' generation, and for generations before theirs, the greatest feats we had accomplished as a nation all involved war. But starting with that night in 1969, the greatest thing my country had ever done was a science and engineering project carried out "for all mankind." This changed our country forever, and forever advanced the edge of what we can accomplish when we work together.

The most recent Astronaut Reunion Dinner I went to included the newest class of astronaut candidates. All of the new recruits were born well after Mike's mission to the Moon—the youngest had been born nineteen years later, in 1988. When I think about the fact that it's been fifty years since Mike and his crewmates accomplished the formerly impossible, I wonder when the promise of that daring will pay off with a mission to Mars. But I also think about these young astronauts preparing to go back to the Moon and beyond. It will be their task to carry the fire lit by Mike and others before him.

PREFACE
to the Third Edition

After the first lunar landing mission in 1969, I got to go on another wonderful adventure. Neil Armstrong, Buzz Aldrin, and I went on an around-the-world trip visiting twenty-two countries. Because we had traveled to the Moon "in peace for all mankind," we expected to be greeted as friends—and we were. But I thought people would say, "Well, you Americans finally did it." But instead, everywhere we went, we heard, "We did it!" All over the globe, people rejoiced that humans had broken gravity's hold and we had walked on another piece of our universe. They felt part of the adventure, and I was amazed by their broad, inclusive, and seemingly unanimous viewpoint.

After the flight some people thought, "Now that we have done that, let's get on with other, more important matters. Why spend all that money on space when we have so many problems here on Earth?" I agree with part of that thinking. We certainly need to do a better job of taking care of our home planet. Seeing its beauty and sensing its fragility from the far-off Moon has made me want to talk and write about the need to protect Earth in the years since Apollo 11.

Today, less than one half of 1 percent of our country's federal budget is devoted to NASA, so 99.5 percent of our money pays for a huge shopping list of solutions and improvements for our country and our planet. I think 99.5 percent is better than 100 percent; I am gratified that support still flows to NASA. Through further explorations in space, I would like us to continue promoting that worldwide spirit of optimism, of cooperation, of a shared bond that we humans found in 1969. I want to see us continue to explore. "Outward-bound," a phrase that can be traced back to the seventeenth century to describe ships about to set sail, for me has always summed up the best of mankind's advances. To look up into the night sky, share its wonder, and realize that we can actually leave Earth and become "outward-bound." To go, to see, to touch, to understand: the Moon, Mars, and beyond: I think our ancestors understood. They were wanderers: Polynesians on rafts, nomads on camels, bushmen on foot—we humans have gone where we have been able to go. We have examined the deepest ocean floors and touched the Moon.

Today NASA wants to return to the Moon, this time to stay. The Moon can be used as a manufacturing center for industries that may eventually be better suited to operating off-Earth. Its ice can be used to provide hydrogen and oxygen, which then could propel rockets to Mars. Beyond Mars, the heavenly bodies known as Europa (a moon of Jupiter) and Enceladus (a moon of Saturn) are of special interest because of their oceans.

I am too old to fly to Mars, and I regret that. But I still think I have been very, very lucky. I was born in the days of biplanes and Buck Rogers, learned to fly in the early jets, and hit my peak when Moon rockets came along. That's hard to beat.

But growing up today can be even more interesting. We now have a much better glimpse of future possibilities than I had in 1969, which I refer to as the Year of the

Moon. It was also a year of great optimism, vitality, and pride. I hope that today's young men and women will take the spirit of '69 and build it into our future space voyages: Outward bound!

FLYING TO THE MOON

AN ASTRONAUT'S STORY

1

Early on the morning of July 20, 1969, I was circling the Moon with Neil Armstrong and Buzz Aldrin in our spacecraft *Columbia*. We had just awakened from a short sleep and were sucking lukewarm coffee out of plastic tubes and munching on bacon that had been squeezed into little cubes, like lumps of sugar. While we were eating our breakfast, we were talking on the radio with our friends in Mission Control in Houston, Texas. Today was the day Neil and Buzz were going to land on the Moon, and Houston was giving them some last-minute advice. Mostly it was technical stuff about their schedule, but all of a sudden they said, "Watch for a lovely girl with a big rabbit. An ancient legend says a beautiful Chinese girl called Chang-O has been living there for four thousand years. It seems she was banished to the Moon because she stole the pill of immortality from her husband. You might also look for her companion, a large Chinese rabbit, who is easy to spot since he is always standing on his hind feet in the shade of a cinnamon tree." Of course, our friends in Houston were kidding, because the Moon doesn't have any cinnamon trees or even any air for people or rabbits to breathe. They probably just wanted to make us laugh a little bit so we wouldn't be too nervous about landing on the Moon for the first time ever.

We *were* a little nervous that morning. We were concerned about how well our spacecraft and computers would work. We also worried about the rocket blast from *Eagle*, our lunar module, which might kick up a lot of dust and prevent Neil Armstrong from being able to see well enough to land. Or suppose Neil couldn't find a spot smooth and level enough to put *Eagle* down? As it turned out, we need not have worried about the Moon, because the *Eagle* landed beautifully in the Sea of

4

Tranquility, and Neil and Buzz were able to walk around and collect some rocks.

The Moon's surface didn't surprise us, because people had studied the Moon very carefully long before Project Apollo came along. In fact, as long as there have been human beings, I suspect that they have wondered about the Moon. How far away was it? How big? What was it made of? How could one visit it? It looked like a shining silver plate hanging in the sky, and on a clear night it seemed almost close enough that a cow could jump over it. But really it is far away—nearly a quarter of a million miles from Earth. Before anyone visited the Moon, scientists made very accurate measurements of its distance. How can you tell how far away something is when you haven't even been there? There are at least two ways. One is to get two people on different sides of the Earth to look at the Moon at the same time and measure where it appears with respect to the stars in the background; that is, which stars appear next to it. By comparing what the two observers see, it is possible to measure an angle— called parallax. Once the parallax angle and the distance between the observers are known, it is possible to draw a triangle and calculate the distance to the Moon:

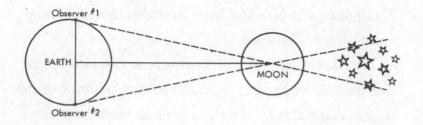

Another way is to bounce a radar signal off the Moon and measure the time it takes the signal to travel from the Earth to the Moon and back again. Since radio waves always travel at the same speed (the speed of light), it is easy to calculate the distance if you know the time. Scientists over the years used both the parallax and the radar methods and got the same answer: 238,000 miles from the Earth to the Moon. That's a long, long way, and yet it took Neil and Buzz and me only three days to get there, so you know we must have been traveling pretty fast.

The reason we were able to go so fast is that we started out riding on a rocket—a huge rocket taller than a football field standing on end. As the rocket's engines blasted away, we left the Earth slowly and then got going faster and faster until finally we had enough speed to overpower the pull of the Earth's gravity. By this time, the rocket had used all its fuel, so we separated from it and floated to the Moon in the weightlessness of space.

Of course, huge rockets weren't invented until fairly recently, and humankind has always wanted to go to the Moon, so you might guess that there were a number of crazy schemes thought up before the rocket came along. My favorite would-be astronaut is Cyrano de Bergerac, a Frenchman who was born four hundred years ago. His idea was to get up early in the morning and gather up dew from his garden. He would put the dew into tiny bottles and strap the bottles to his body. Then, when the morning sun's heat caused the dew to evaporate, he would float up with it—to the Moon.

Another famous Frenchman was Jules Verne, who was born almost two hundred years ago. His idea was to shoot a moonship out of a huge cannon, which he called the *Columbiad*. Verne wrote a fascinating make-believe story about a trip to the Moon, and many of his ideas came close to the way the Apollo flights actually took place. For example, as a location for his *Columbiad*, he picked, of all places on Earth, Tampa, Florida—just a few miles west of Cape Canaveral, the launching pad for our *Columbia*.

As I circled the Moon in July of 1969, I was thinking about Armstrong and Aldrin, not de Bergerac and Verne. Okay, so we were 238,000 miles from Earth—that much I knew—but what would Neil and Buzz find on the surface? No one had ever been there before, and I was worried, even though we did have a lot of information to help us. Ever since Galileo first peered at the Moon through his telescope more than four hundred years ago, we had been gathering facts about its pockmarked surface. We had photographs of it, and maps too. We had crashed into it with our Ranger unmanned spacecraft and even soft-landed a Surveyor spacecraft loaded with instruments. We knew it had no atmosphere and we knew its surface could be either colder than Siberia in January or hotter than the Sahara Desert in August. Whether any one spot on its surface was hot or cold depended on its angle to the Sun. The Moon does not spin, but keeps one side pointed toward the Earth as it makes a gigantic orbit around the Earth.

It takes the Moon one month to go around the Earth once. In the meantime, the Earth is making an even bigger (*much* bigger) orbit around the Sun. What all this means is that in a month's time a spot on the Moon's surface will be exposed to every possible condition of lighting—from inky black to sunlight directly overhead ("noon"). Months before our flight, scientists had picked a landing spot that looked nice and smooth. Then they figured out what time of the month we should arrive at that spot. We wanted Neil and Buzz to be able to see well, with the Sun behind them as they descended, and we wanted them not to get too hot, so we decided that landing just after dawn would be best. As you look at the full Moon, if you use your imagination, you can see the face of the Man in the Moon. Neil and Buzz would be landing just below his left eye. On the day they landed, his left eye was barely visible and his right eye was in darkness. In other words, the people on Earth would see slightly less than a half moon.

Remember that the Moon produces no light of its own, but merely bounces back sunlight that hits its surface, so you can tell the direction of the Sun by looking at the Moon.

The Moon always has one half lighted and one half dark. The reason it looks different to us is that, as it goes around the Earth in its circular orbit, its angle to the Sun keeps changing, and sometimes we see only the light side ("full moon") or only the dark side ("new moon") or half and half ("half moon") or mostly dark ("crescent moon"). When I was young, I only thought a little bit about why the Moon seemed to change shape as the month wore on, and I *never* thought about what the Earth would look like when seen from the Moon. The planet Earth produces no light of its own but merely reflects sunlight, just as the Moon does. Sure enough, coming back from the Moon, I could look out my spacecraft window and see a crescent Earth.

The Moon is not nearly as large as the Earth, and therefore its gravity is not as strong. Any object, such as a human body, is attracted more strongly to a large planet than to a small one. On Earth I weigh 165 pounds, but on the Moon I would weigh only 27 pounds. Imagine a grown man weighing 27 pounds! That is why Neil and Buzz were able to jump around like kangaroos on the Moon, even though they were loaded down with heavy equipment. Now, on the surface of Jupiter, which is the largest planet in our solar system, I would weigh 436 pounds. A person would have a difficult time standing up on Jupiter, much less jumping.

Before we got to the Moon we had a pretty good idea of what we would find—rocks, and more rocks. We knew this from photographs taken on Earth through telescopes, and also those taken by spacecraft from up close. Neil and Buzz should have brought a small piece of green cheese with them from Earth, just so they could say they had brought some green cheese back from the Moon. In addition to being all rocks, another bad thing about the

Moon is that there is no air to breathe. We didn't think there was any water either, although we weren't too sure about that. With no air or water, the Moon would be a very difficult place for humans to live, or even visit. Neil and Buzz carried their own breathing supply of oxygen in packs on their backs. If someone wanted to live on the Moon more or less permanently, that person would probably have to put up a plastic bubble, fill it with air, and stay inside it. The Moon would be a great place to observe the stars because there is no atmosphere to get in the way and block the view. On Earth, we think we can see the stars clearly, but we really can't. Over 90 percent of the energy coming from the stars is blocked out by our atmosphere and never reaches the ground. On the Moon, with no atmosphere, astronomers would not have this problem, and they would be able to learn a lot more about our universe.

Of course, it's going to be a long, long time before astronomers or anyone else begins to live on the Moon inside a bubble. It would be very complicated and expensive to get all the necessary equipment up there. It took us eight years from the time President John F. Kennedy said we should go to the Moon until Neil stepped on it. It took me six years of training as a NASA astronaut to learn everything I needed to know to make the trip. That is a long time to study, especially when you know you have only one chance to pass the final exam. But along the way I learned a lot of fascinating things, like how to find food in the jungle or what to do about chiggers, and I would like to tell you about some of them.

2

I first became interested in flying when I was about nine years old. I was living in San Antonio, Texas, and there were several airfields nearby. I used to wonder what it would be like to sit in a cockpit way up there, high above the green fields, and make the airplane go wherever I wanted. The first model airplane I ever made was of a famous racing plane called the Gee Bee. It had short wings and a fat, stubby fuselage with a huge engine in front. It looked sort of like a bumblebee, with a tiny cockpit perched way back where the vertical tail joined the fuselage. Only a few Gee Bees were built, and they must have been very tricky to fly; eventually they all crashed. I carved the model out of balsa wood and painted it in red and white racing colors. On the sides of the fuselage I added its insignia, a "lucky" pair of dice. The Gee Bee could fly a circular course at over 250 miles an hour, which is slow today, but in those days seemed plenty fast.

I got my first airplane ride when I was eleven, and the pilot even let me fly the plane a little bit. It was a twin-engined seaplane called a Grumman Widgeon (a widgeon is a kind of duck). I found it was very difficult to keep the plane going straight. The secret was keeping your eyes glued to the horizon and noticing whether the nose of the plane was creeping up above or falling below the horizon. If the nose fell, you were supposed to pull back slightly on the wheel, and vice versa. The more trouble I had, the more the pilot laughed! I was sort of embarrassed at the time, but when the flight was over, I realized that I had really liked it, and wanted to do it again. However, World War II started about then, and I wasn't able to fly again for a long time. Of course, during the war I read a lot about flying, especially about our fighter planes, which were shooting down the enemy. My favorite plane was the British Spitfire, which was a beautiful, graceful-looking airplane with a slender fuselage and a curved, elliptical-shaped wing.

After World War II, when the jet age started, I was a student in college, at West Point. When I graduated, I had a choice to become either an Army or Air Force officer. I decided to go into the Air Force and give flying a try. I was worried about this decision, because if I flunked out of flying school I still had to stay in the Air Force, and I thought that for a non-flier the Army would be a better career than the Air Force.

I got my first fright when I reported to flying school and flunked my eye exam. I could see fine off in the distance, but up close I flunked—just barely. The Air Force doctors gave me a second chance and scheduled me for another exam a week later. I immediately consulted a civilian eye doctor, and he gave me some eye exercises to do, and I passed the second exam. Whew!

Then the flying began, and that was really fun. I flew a North American T-6 Texan. It was a yellow two-seater with a 450-horsepower radial engine, a low wing, and retractable landing gear. Generally I sat in the front seat, with my instructor directly behind me. When I did something wrong, which was often, he would yell and scream at me over the interphone, and I would get very nervous. The more nervous I got, the tighter I would clutch the control stick, and at the end of an hour my right arm would ache. I also worried because I am left-handed, and I had to learn to fly with my right hand, since I had to control the throttle with my left (it was way over on the left side). Gradually, however, I learned to relax, and I found that being left-handed didn't really make any difference. Between screams my instructor told me I was doing fine (I guess he just liked to scream), and I got to feeling fairly confident and at home in the airplane. At least I didn't have one problem that bothered a lot of my fellow students: airsickness. Flying in a plane just makes some people sick. Most of them get over it after a couple of weeks, but some never do, and they have to be "washed out" of pilot training.

After about twenty hours of practice with my instructor, he decided I was ready to fly solo. My first flight by myself was a little bit scary, but I found I really enjoyed being up there all alone with no one yelling at me. I never guessed that one day I would be flying solo around the Moon, and enjoying that, too. However, learning to fly solo is just the beginning. Flying can be very complicated: to do it properly, one must learn to fly at night, and in bad weather, and in formation with other planes. All this takes a long time, and it was nine months before I was finished with the T-6 and ready to try jets.

In some ways a jet is easier to fly than a plane with a piston engine and a propeller. With a prop, if you change power abruptly, the nose veers to one side or the other. Called torque, this reaction must be compensated for by your feet pushing on the rudder pedals. With a jet engine there is no torque, so your feet are not nearly as busy and you can concentrate on other things. On the other hand, when you want power from a piston engine, the engine responds as soon as your hand moves the throttle. With a jet, especially the early jets, there may be a lag of ten or more seconds from the time you decide you need extra power until the engine finally speeds up enough to give it to you. This lag can be very embarrassing if, for example, you have waited until the last minute to realize that you are going to land short of the runway. In a jet you have to think further ahead.

The first jet I flew was called a T-33. Built by Lockheed, it was a two-seat version of the Shooting Star, which was designed during the closing days of World War II. The US Air Force retired its last NT-33—a modified version of the T-33—in 1997. Some T-33s are still flying today, over sixty years later, indicating that its basic design was excellent. The T-33 could climb up to almost 50,000 feet and could go nearly 600 miles an hour. It carried enough fuel to stay up for three hours, but its ejection seat was very uncomfortable and my backside got numb long before two hours had passed. I didn't envy people who stayed up in bombers or transports nearly a whole day. Nor did I think about how long it might take to fly to the Moon. I just wanted to be a jet fighter pilot. Jets like the T-33 are smoother than prop planes, and more fun to fly.

When I got my wings, after a most enjoyable year of flight training, I also got some great news. I was not only going to be a fighter pilot, but I was going to Las Vegas, Nevada, where training was given in the very best fighter, the F-86 Sabrejet. At that time (1953) the Sabres were battling the MiGs in Korea, and doing it very successfully. More than anything, I wanted to fly the sleek, swept-wing supersonic F-86, and I was delighted when I got my chance. Although trickier to fly than the Shooting Star, it was also more fun, it had only one seat, and above all, you knew it was the best. We new pilots felt honored to have a chance to master it, and we worked hard to learn as much as we could as fast as we could. Unfortunately, a few of my friends were killed in the process. Today, flying is a lot safer, especially on airliners, but fighters have always been more difficult, especially in the early jet days.

After graduating from Las Vegas, I flew the F-86 for four years, accumulating over a thousand flying hours in it. I got to see some interesting parts of the world from the cockpit of an F-86, all the way from the Mexican border to the eastern Mediterranean Sea. I saw the Libyan Desert, where nomads tend their camels as they did a thousand years ago. I saw pieces of the great Greenland glacier cracking and falling into the sea to make icebergs. I saw the lush green of Ireland, and the bright blue sea of the Greek islands, and the yellow gray haze of industrialized Germany. I saw Paris and London and Rome. I saw foreign places and met people whose viewpoints were different from mine. I liked being an Air Force pilot. My sister's husband was a pilot also, but he was a *test* pilot. His work, flying all kinds of new airplanes, sounded even better than what I was doing with my old F-86. So I went back to school, something I had never expected to do again, to learn how to be a test pilot, at the Air Force Test Pilot School at Edwards Air Force Base, California.

Fortunately, in high school and college I had taken a fair number of math and science courses, because now I needed them to understand how airplanes *really* flew, and what made the difference between a good airplane and a bad one. I had never thought about *that* before. By the time I had gotten my hands on an airplane, the test pilots had already wrung it out and had made sure that it was safe for me to fly. Now *I* had that responsibility, to check everything from A to Z, so that when a new airplane entered squadron service, there would be no surprises waiting for the new graduate, the inexperienced second lieutenant. At the Test Pilot School I learned how to get as much information as possible from a new airplane in the shortest possible time. When I graduated, I stayed on at Edwards Air Force Base, and was assigned to the Fighter Test section. This was exactly what I wanted, but I was a little disappointed because at that time there weren't any new fighters to test. Instead, I spent my time flying older planes that were being modified in various ways. It was interesting flying, and I got a chance to fly such airplanes as the North American F-100 Super Sabre, the Convair F-102 Delta Dagger, the Lockheed F-104 Starfighter, and quite a few others.

I really liked my job as a test pilot; in fact, I thought it was the best possible job I could have, except for one thing. There were other people going a lot higher and faster than I was. They were called astronauts, and they had been picked from the ranks of test pilots. There were only seven, and I didn't know any of them, but some of my test pilot friends did and told me stories about them. I was surprised to hear that they weren't supermen at all, but just test pilots (admittedly, a bit older and more experienced) who made mistakes just like the rest of us. I wondered what it would take to become an astronaut.

The Air Force must have been wondering the same thing too, because at this time they renamed the Test Pilot School something much fancier—the Aerospace Research Pilot School. They also began teaching space courses, and they invited me to come back to the school to take some of them. So I became a student once again, and learned about what keeps satellites in orbit, and about how weightlessness affects the human body, and about how to fly machines without wings. After graduating I went back to my old job in Fighter Test, and waited until the Space Agency decided they needed some more astronauts. I only had a couple of months to wait before NASA announced it was going to hire a third group of astronauts. I had tried the year before to become a NASA astronaut and had been rejected, but this time I was hopeful—because of the space courses I had taken—that I knew more than before, and that NASA would take me.

The first thing I had to do was pass a physical exam that took a whole week. It was not a pleasant week, because I worried the entire time that they would find something wrong with me. Also, some of the tests were not pleasant. They took what seemed like a quart of my blood, poured cold water in my ears (which makes you dizzy), and performed a lot of other tests that I didn't even understand. They checked the condition of my heart by making me walk on a treadmill that they adjusted to get steeper and steeper as the minutes went by. They stopped the treadmill when my heartbeat got up to 180 beats per minute, which is pretty fast. I also took written mental tests and had interviews with psychiatrists. Some of the questions seemed strange, like "Are you a slob or a snob?" You had to pick one or the other. I picked "snob," although I don't think I am one. Somehow I didn't want to pick "slob."

After a week in San Antonio, Texas, where the physical exam took place, I went to Houston for an interview. It was conducted by Deke Slayton and Alan Shepard, two of the original seven astronauts, and some other technical experts. The questions were designed to see how much we knew about NASA's plans for flying in space, and to determine what we might contribute, based on our experience as pilots. I had studied a lot about Gemini and Apollo, the two spacecraft that were supposed to fly next (after Mercury), and I thought I gave good answers to most of the questions. But some I did not know; for example, I knew practically nothing about the Atlas booster, which was used to put a Mercury spacecraft into orbit. Incidentally, the astronauts always called their machines spacecraft, not capsules. Capsules were something you swallowed.

I went back to Edwards Air Force Base after the interview and began the long wait to hear whether I would be rejected again. I figured this was my last chance, because I was just one year below the age limit of thirty-four, and I thought it would be years and years before NASA would pick any more astronauts. They already had sixteen—the original seven plus a second group of nine.

After a month of waiting and worrying, I got a phone call from Deke Slayton. He said they would take me, if I still wanted to work for NASA. If I still wanted to? He must have been kidding—I had been thinking about nothing else for the whole month. Deke didn't sound the slightest bit excited, but I certainly was, and so was my wife, Patricia, when I told her. She also had been nervous during the long wait. Our oldest child, Kate, was only four years old, too young to understand what was happening. I soon found out that NASA had selected fourteen of us. These men would all become close friends in the coming years. They were a grand group of people, easy to live and work with, and I enjoyed being with them. Their names were Buzz Aldrin, Bill Anders, Charlie Bassett, Al Bean, Gene Cernan, Roger Chaffee, Walt Cunningham, Donn Eisele, Ted Freeman, Dick Gordon, Rusty Schweickart, Dave Scott, and C. C. Williams. And, oh yes, I almost forgot, Mike Collins. Of this group of fourteen, three would orbit the Earth, three would orbit the Moon, four would walk on the Moon, and four would get killed. There is a lot of luck in this life.

3

My wife and children and I moved to Houston in January of 1964. NASA was building a new center there, called the Manned Spacecraft Center. The astronauts' offices were being moved into a brand-new building and I was assigned my own small office, with a big gray metal desk, several large bookcases, and a small blackboard on one wall. Inside the desk there were lots of pencils, a ruler, and several yellow pads of paper. That was all the equipment you needed to become an astronaut, or at least to start becoming an astronaut.

No one told me how I should be spending every minute of every day; I had to decide that for myself. I decided to begin by learning as much as I could about the history of the space program, about Projects Mercury, Gemini, and Apollo, and to find out what was bothering the engineers who were designing the spacecraft of the future.

One nice thing about studying the space program in 1964 was that it was quite new, and one didn't have to go back very far in the history books to learn about it. Of course, people like Jules Verne (and how many before him?) had been dreaming of flying to the Moon for centuries, and the Chinese had had small rockets for seven hundred years. But it had only been fairly recently that humankind had begun to think seriously about using rocket power to leave the surface of the Earth. Piston and jet engines are of no use in space, because they require air to operate (to mix with the fuel before burning) and there is no air above the Earth's atmosphere, in the vacuum of space. A rocket solves this problem by carrying everything it needs with it—not only fuel but also the oxidizer needed to mix with the fuel and cause it to burn. It was the twentieth century before people thought seriously about this, and there were three men who seemed to be ahead of everyone else in the world.

The first was a Russian by the name of Konstantin Tsiolkovsky, who was born in 1857. After a childhood illness left Tsiolkovsky almost totally deaf, schools refused him admission, so he chose to educate himself. He spent so much time studying on his own at the public library in Moscow that he was given a job as a schoolteacher. In his free time he designed a wide variety of airships and spacecraft. None of them ever flew, but their theoretical possibilities were very far advanced. For example, he thought plants should be grown aboard spacecraft, to purify the air. When people finally decide to live in space, I expect that they may do exactly what Tsiolkovsky recommended and use plants to produce oxygen for the crew to breathe. The crew will return the favor by exhaling carbon dioxide, which (along with sunlight and water) plants need to live. Scientists, who love to give long names to things, call this process photosynthesis.

Konstantin Tsiolkovsky died in 1935, and the Russians made a museum out of his house. I visited there once and talked to Tsiolkovsky's grandson. Visitors not only can learn a lot about Tsiolkovsky's plans for flying into space but can also see how he lived on Earth. Even his bicycle has been saved, and the tin ear trumpet, nearly two feet long, that Konstantin used to hold up to his ear for his students to speak into.

In the United States the great pioneer of rocketry was Robert Hutchings Goddard, who was born in Massachusetts in 1882—the same year my dad was born. One day when he was seventeen, Goddard was up in a cherry tree, trimming the branches, when he suddenly thought how wonderful it would be to make a machine that could ascend all the way to Mars. He didn't know how to do it, but when he climbed down from that tree he felt he was a different boy. Life now had a purpose for him. Goddard realized that to fulfill that purpose he needed to get an education, and he pursued his studies all the way to a PhD degree. Unlike Tsiolkovsky, who concentrated on theory, Goddard built rockets. In 1926, he flew the world's first *liquid*-rocket-propelled vehicle (whereas the Chinese and others had used *solid* propellants, not unlike the Fourth of July variety). The more successful Goddard's rockets became, the more noise they made. Finally the police got so many complaints from his neighbors that they told him he couldn't shoot off any more rockets *in that neighborhood*. Goddard solved the problem by moving to the desert near Roswell, New Mexico, where he could fire his rockets in peace. They only went up to about 9,000 feet, but that was still better than anyone else in the world could do in the nineteen-thirties. They were the ancestors of the gigantic Saturn V Moon rocket.

The third rocket genius was a German named Hermann Oberth. He figured out the mathematical equations that proved space flight was practical. His ideas also led to the founding of an organization called the Society for Spaceship Travel. Its members tried experimenting with small liquid-propelled rockets, which were generally recovered by parachutes. In World War II, Germany built on Oberth's ideas and developed the V-2, a rocket powerful enough to carry an explosive warhead all the way from northern Germany to London. After World War II, Wernher von Braun, the leader of this effort, came to the United States with some of his experts and began building rockets in this country. Their work did not receive much attention until October 4, 1957, when the Russians launched Sputnik, the first man-made satellite in history. Sputnik came as a great shock to the world, because (despite Tsiolkovsky's work) Russia was considered to be a backward nation, especially in the area of advanced technology. Sputnik weighed 184 pounds, and it obviously required a very large rocket to accelerate this mass to a sufficient speed to achieve orbit. The United States couldn't even put a flea into orbit, much less 184 pounds, but people like von Braun were working on it, and when they heard about the Russian success, they started working even harder. The space race was on!

Early in 1958, the United States put up its first satellite, Explorer I, and it wasn't long before people started talking about putting a person into orbit. Project Mercury was designed to do that, but again the Russians got there first, and put the first human being into orbit. In 1961, Yuri Gagarin made one circle around the Earth in 89 minutes. Yuri was a very personable young man, friendly, with a big smile, and he became a hero in Russia and a celebrity in all parts of the world. He was killed flying a MiG-15 jet trainer in 1968.

Alan Shepard was the first American in space, followed closely by Gus Grissom. Their two flights were not intended to go into orbit but simply to fly a ballistic arc up a bit more than one hundred miles and then fall back down into the sea. John Glenn was the first Mercury astronaut to circle the Earth, making three orbits. Then came Scott Carpenter and Wally Schirra, and finally

Gordon Cooper finished up the Mercury program in May 1963, staying in space for thirty-four hours.

The Mercury astronauts were allowed to name their spacecraft. All the names ended with a 7, since there were but seven astronauts in existence, and they wanted to emphasize their unity. The names they picked were Freedom 7, Liberty Bell 7, Friendship 7, Aurora 7, Sigma 7, and Faith 7. An aurora is a group of flashing lights in the sky, usually seen only on clear nights in the far north. Sigma is one of the letters of the Greek alphabet used frequently in mathematics to indicate the sum of various parts. In this case I guess it indicated the sum of all the work that many people put into the launch of a manned spacecraft.

Between Cooper's flight in 1963 and my arrival in Houston in 1964, there had been no more space flights. A second group of nine astronauts had been picked, and now my group of fourteen, so there were thirty of us instead of seven, and we were all eager to fly in space, especially we rookies. The reason none of us was doing so was that Project Mercury had ended and Project Gemini had not yet begun. In a speech to Congress, President Kennedy had said (shortly after Alan Shepard's flight in

1961), "that this nation should commit itself to achieving the goal, before this decade is out, of landing a man on the Moon and returning him safely to the Earth." We all had that goal in mind already, but the problem was there were a number of questions that had to be answered before we could try a lunar trip. The two-man Gemini spacecraft was being designed to find out as much as we could in Earth orbit before trying to take an Apollo spacecraft all the way to the Moon.

The biggest unknown was what would happen to a person who stayed weightless for a long time. Some doctors thought the heart and blood-supply system would become confused by the lack of gravity and would not function properly. It is not possible to create weightlessness here on Earth, except for very short periods of time. One way would be to jump off a tall building, in which case you would be weightless until you hit the ground. I don't recommend that! A second way, which we did try, was to dive down in a speeding jet until it got going very fast, pull up abruptly into a steep climb, and then push over into a lazy arc in the shape of a parabola. For approximately twenty seconds near the top of the arc, you and your plane would be weightless. Those twenty seconds were the most experience we had, until Mercury began with Alan Shepard's fifteen-minute flight. Then the flights got longer, until finally Cooper stayed up nearly a day and a half, with no apparent ill effects. But a round trip to the Moon would take *over a week*, and no one was willing to guarantee that a person's body wouldn't somehow be damaged by being weightless that long. Also, the Russian cosmonauts were reported to be having some problems with nausea. Therefore, Gemini was created to find out once and for all, by keeping two men up for fourteen days. Of course, this long flight would be undertaken only if no harm came to the astronauts on the earlier Gemini flights, which were scheduled to stay up for four days, and then eight days.

The second most important unknown was the question of rendezvous and docking. The Apollo machinery was being designed with two separate spacecraft, which would rendezvous and dock with each other while in orbit around the Moon. But no one had ever made a space rendezvous or docking! Was it practical to plan Apollo that way? Could two vehicles speeding around Earth or the Moon really find each other, get into the same orbit at the same speed, and gently bring their two craft together? Could they do it *every time* they tried, or only when they were lucky? We had to know these things, as well as the effects of weightlessness on the human body, before we could safely obey President Kennedy's order to get to the Moon by the end of the decade.

A third thing we hoped to learn from Project Gemini was how to operate *outside* a spacecraft. We wanted people to walk on the airless Moon, not just to land and stay inside their spacecraft, and that meant that experience had to be gained working inside a pressure suit containing its own atmosphere. Of course, we couldn't "Moon walk" during Gemini, but we could "space walk" and find out how to design portable breathing and cooling equipment.

In addition to these questions, which we hoped Gemini would answer, there were also a number of hazards involved in going to the Moon. For one thing, it was simply a long way off, and that meant all our machinery had to be very reliable. If something broke in Earth orbit, we could probably be on the ground within an hour. But if the same thing happened on the Moon, it might take three days to get home. For example, every once in a while the Sun releases a burst of deadly energy, called a solar flare. These particles speed out from the Sun, and would go right on through the walls of a spacecraft and the bodies of the astronauts. If severe enough, a solar flare could cause the crew to become sick and perhaps even die. Here on the surface of the Earth, we are protected against solar flares by our atmosphere, which prevents most of the radiation from reaching the ground. Meteorites are another source of worry. In 1964, we didn't know how many of them there were in space, or what to do if one hit a spacecraft, but we did know from studying the Moon that meteorites in the past had caused millions of craters (some of them huge) as they struck the Moon.

The Moon's surface also was the subject of great debate in 1964. Some people thought that, except for a few boulders, it would be hard and flat—and they turned out to be right. But other scientists thought there was a layer of dust on the surface that in places might be thirty or forty feet thick! If a spacecraft came down there, it would be in great trouble, sinking out of sight. Other scientists thought that static electricity would cause whatever dust there was to cling to the windows of the spacecraft, blocking the astronauts' view and causing them to crash on landing.

Other people worried about the zone of constant sunlight between the Earth and the Moon. In Earth orbit, a spacecraft hides from the Sun for a portion of each orbit, when it is in the Earth's shadow (we call that *night*). But on the way to the Moon there is no place to hide, and the sunlight is continuous, twenty-four hours a day. Wouldn't the side of the spacecraft facing the Sun get too hot, and the side in the shade get too cold? What would it be like inside under these conditions? No one knew whether it would be too hot or too cold inside. Also, what would the humidity be? If it got too moist, we were afraid that the moisture would condense on the coldest equipment, just as a pitcher of ice tea on a hot summer day gets dripping wet on the outside. We didn't want that to happen anywhere near our electronic equipment, because the moisture might cause short circuits, which in turn would cause our radios to fail.

Radio failure was especially worrisome, because if the astronauts couldn't talk to anybody they would have to do all the navigating back from the Moon without help from radar tracking stations and computers on Earth. Navigation instruments were being designed, but no one really knew how accurate they would be, and they had to be very, very precise. For example, as it approaches the Earth, a spacecraft returning from the Moon must be within a very narrow zone about forty miles high. If it misses this zone on the high side, it will skip the Earth entirely and keep on going past; on the low side, it will hit the atmosphere at too steep an angle and burn up. Hitting a forty-mile target from a distance of 238,000 miles is about like trying to split a human hair with a razor blade thrown from a distance of twenty feet.

My gray desk began to fill up with papers and my shelves with books as I learned more and more about all these problems. In addition to reading on my own, I attended a school that had been arranged especially for us "new guys"—the third group of astronauts. I'm not fond of schools generally, but I thought this was a good one, for several reasons. First, there were no grades, and that is always nice. Second, it was only a few hours a day for a couple of months. And third, I figured this was the last school I would ever have to attend. We studied a number of subjects, some complicated and some simple. We studied astronomy, aerodynamics, rocket propulsion, meteorology, guidance and navigation, and computers—to name just a few. We also studied a lot of geology, which I didn't expect. Geology is the study of the origin, history, and structure of the Earth. Since the Earth is made up mostly of rocks, geology is mostly the study of rocks. We didn't have any Moon rocks to study, so we studied Earth rocks instead. The idea was that if and when we finally reached the Moon we would have a much better idea of what to look for, and what kinds of rocks would be best to bring back.

Houston in 1964 was an exciting if somewhat strange place. Granted, studying rocks wasn't exactly thrilling, but look where it might lead! A space walk? A Moon walk? Who knew? Even if I never got to the Moon, I was finally an ASTRONAUT*!!★-WOW! Now I just had to get assigned to a space flight.

4

Before I could fly in space, however, there were still a thousand things I had to learn. Some of them I could absorb while sitting in my little office in Houston, but others required trips to far-off places. For example, in our study of geology, we could only learn so much by looking at rocks in a laboratory. Beyond that, we had to see those rocks in place, to appreciate how they had been formed. Craters on the Moon can be caused either by the impact of meteorites or by volcanic action. To recognize the differences between the two, we studied an impact crater in Arizona and volcanoes in

Hawaii. We visited other unusual rock formations in Oregon, New Mexico, and Texas—and even spent one night at the bottom of the Grand Canyon.

The Grand Canyon trip was the first geology trip I took, and it was also the most impressive. The Canyon was created by the Colorado River flowing through the Arizona desert and digging an ever-deepening trench, which is now nearly a mile deep and many miles across. As you walk down a narrow pathway that zigzags back and forth, you can see the history of the region in the various layers of rocks. The young rocks are on top, but as the river digs deeper, it exposes older and older layers. The age of some rocks at the bottom of the Canyon has been estimated at over two billion years. Not million, but billion. That is nearly half as old as we believe our solar system to be. The trees and plants also change greatly as you descend the Grand Canyon. There is one zone, high up in the shadows, that is cool enough to allow the growth of fir trees usually found only much farther north. Then, near the bottom, there are cactuses of the same variety found in the deserts to the south. It is quite a contrast of rocks and plants, like a slice of Canada piled on top of a piece of Mexico. The animals are equally varied, ranging from mountain goats to horned toads. Not to mention the burros, the most stubborn creature known to man. These burros were not wild ones, but had saddles on them, and we rode them back up the Canyon wall after spending the night in an inn at the bottom.

I picked my burro because he looked young and strong and eager, but he was the worst loafer in the bunch. Every time I stopped kicking him, he stopped walking, so I got more exercise riding him up than I had the day before from walking down.

In addition to geology, there were a number of other reasons for us to take trips. For example, we were concerned that one of our spacecraft might have to get back on the ground in a big hurry and might come down in a remote area of the ocean or the jungle or the desert. We didn't have to worry about very cold regions, because, whether returning from Earth orbit or from the Moon, our flight path stayed near the equator, where the climate is warm. If we came down unexpectedly in the ocean, we had no choice but to stay with the spacecraft until rescued, but in the desert or jungle there are a lot of ways to keep alive, and they had to be learned.

To learn about the jungle, we spent nearly two weeks in Panama. The first couple of days we spent in a classroom, studying an Air Force manual designed to help pilots who made emergency landings in unfamiliar places. I thought the manual itself was kind of strange. It started by saying, "Anything that creeps, crawls, swims, or flies is a possible source of food." While I was thinking that statement over, it went on to say, "People eat grasshoppers, hairless caterpillars, ant eggs, and termites." Ugh! You'd have to be pretty hungry to eat a caterpillar, with or without hair. Couldn't we please find something a little nicer to eat? The manual continues: "Look on the ground for hedgehogs . . . porcupines . . . mice . . . wild pigs; in the trees for bats, squirrels, rats, and monkeys." Anyone for mouse pie, bat stew, porcupine soup, or squirrel soufflé? Apparently there is no peanut butter and jelly in the jungle. About the only advice from the manual with which I agreed a hundred percent was "Don't eat toads." Now *that* was a promise I didn't have any trouble keeping!

In addition to animals that could be hunted for food, the manual mentioned others that should be avoided: "Tigers, rhinoceroses, elephants—are rarely seen and best left alone . . . Avoid many-legged insects . . . Scorpions are real pests, for they like to hide in clothes, bedding, or shoes." I can just see it now, getting up in the morning and looking for a dozen scorpions. Let's see. Here's one in each shoe, two in my hip pocket, three trying to hide in my hairbrush. I wonder what happened to the rest of the gang. Oops! There's one now, trying to sneak into my box of waterproof matches—and another, peeking out from the arm of my sweater!

As these thoughts ran through my mind, I decided that the classroom wasn't such a bad place after all. There were plenty of scorpions and snakes here, but they were all dead, floating in bottles filled with alcohol. After a couple of days, our instructors decided it was time to *see* the real jungle, not just talk about it, so they loaded us into helicopters and landed us in a small jungle clearing. We were to spend three days by ourselves, in teams of two, learning to live off the land.

My partner was Bill Anders, and he was great, because he knew a lot about camping. He had been a Boy Scout (I had not) and he loved to hike to remote fishing spots, in hopes of catching big trout from places no one else had been. Bill was also a finicky eater, which was nice too, as I will explain later. Our first job was to hike a couple of miles through the jungle to our assigned camping area. On the way I was really surprised—the jungle seemed empty. Where were all the hedgehogs, porcupines, pangolins, mice, and wild pigs we had heard about? Was it possible for a jungle to be empty? Not even a bird chirped. Maybe we were making such tremendous noise as we crashed through the underbrush that even the oldest, slowest hedgehog was able to keep far ahead of us. In any case, what were we going to eat? Bill said he wasn't hungry, but I sure was, and as night fell and the mosquitoes came out, I lay in my hammock, listened to my stomach gurgle, and felt sorry for myself. I was supposed to be on my way to the Moon instead of fooling around in the middle of an empty jungle.

The next morning I tried to catch some fish that I could see in a nearby stream. They were just minnows, but they looked edible, and I would have loved to eat thirty or forty of them for breakfast. But no such luck, and I wasted a couple of hours before I gave up, hungrier than ever. Bill and I decided that if we couldn't catch any animals to eat, we should try for an edible plant of some sort. Palm trees were the only things around that we knew for sure were okay to eat, because our instructors had told us so. The part that you ate was called the heart, and it was a pale green crunchy stalk somewhat larger than a celery stalk. The only problem was that the heart of palm was inside the tree, and first you had to chop down the tree and cut it open. Furthermore, some varieties of palm tree had edible hearts and some didn't. Unless you were a real expert, the only way to find out which was which was to chop one down and see for yourself. With just a small dull machete apiece, that would be a lot of work. Bill and I talked it over and decided it was our only chance for food, so we picked a likely-looking tree and started chopping. After what seemed like hours, it finally toppled to the ground. As soon as it did, ants began to pour out of it, and we could see that it was not a healthy tree inside, although it looked fine outside. The heart was discolored and looked rotten. The ants were everywhere, angrily running around looking for an enemy—us! We retreated, disgusted with our bad luck (or lack of skill in tree selection), and discussed what to do next. We finally decided that if we wanted to eat, we had no choice but to try another palm tree. We picked a second one with great care and started hacking away. This time we hit the jackpot. When it finally fell, we could tell right away that the heart looked good, with not a single ant in sight. We cut out a piece of the tender heart, which was nearly two feet long and about five inches in diameter. Now we had enough salad to last for days. Of course, we didn't have any dressing to put on the heart of palm, but we just munched it plain and raw, like chewing dry, tough celery. It wasn't bad, with a flavor that reminded me a little bit of nuts, lettuce, and artichokes all mixed together.

That evening our instructors took pity on us and gave us something else to eat: chunks of iguana. An iguana is a large lizard, and looks fearsome, very much like a miniature dragon. Actually, it is a shy, harmless creature. If I had not been so hungry, I might have felt bad about eating one, but instead I was delighted to half fill a large tin can with water from the stream and throw in the iguana cut into pieces the size of small fists. We built a roaring fire and propped the can up over the coals. Pretty soon our makeshift pot was bubbling away, and the smell coming from it was actually delicious. It didn't smell like an ugly old lizard at all. When it cooled down enough to taste, I tried a bite. It was good: tender flesh, with a taste somewhat like chicken, but still quite different. Bill Anders, however, wasn't too happy about eating what to us seemed such a strange creature, and stuck to heart of palm. He graciously gave me his share of the iguana. That evening I sat close to the fire (which kept the pesky mosquitoes away), munching heart of palm and slurping down great chunks of iguana. Although it's not polite, I burped loudly a couple of times, feeling quite contented. With a full stomach, I thought the jungle didn't seem like a bad place at all.

The next day we met an Indian chief named Antonio. He was a friend of our instructors, and through an interpreter he told us a little about his life in the jungle. He was forty years old and a grandfather, he told us, but he looked much, much younger. He was short, with jet-black hair and a lean, muscular body. He wore only a loincloth; somehow mosquitoes didn't seem to bite him, or if they did, their bites didn't bother him. His face was unlined and he seemed completely carefree, not like the forty-year-old men I knew, most of whom lived in big American cities. I saw Antonio once again, years later in Washington, D.C. It felt odd to see him there, all dressed up in city clothes, just as I surely seemed to him out of place in the jungle.

In addition to our jungle trip, we also spent a couple of days living in the desert, but that wasn't as much fun. If your spacecraft comes down in the desert, about all you can do is find a shady place and wait to be rescued. Water is all-important; with plenty to drink, you can survive for weeks; without it, you will be dead within a couple of days, no matter how determined or brave or intelligent you may be. The day I was dropped off in the desert, the sand temperature was 148° Fahrenheit, but my partner, Charlie Bassett, and I were able to dig into the side of a sandy hill and scoop out a shady spot that was a lot cooler than 148°. We also made our own clothes, from parachute cloth. Deciding what to wear is one problem that a downed airman never has, because he always has a parachute with him, with yards and yards of nylon material that can be made into trousers or jackets or sleeping bags or even tents. Charlie and I made hats and long, flowing gowns, trying to imitate Arabs, but I expect we looked more like little kids wearing their mothers' party gowns than like Arabs. But, anyway, the clothes kept us from getting sunburned, and they did help to decrease the rate at which we were perspiring. In the desert, the faster you perspire, the quicker you die, if you don't have anything to drink. We were given a small amount of water, which helped, but we were quite thirsty when we were finally "rescued" and returned to civilization, which in this case turned out to be Reno, Nevada.

For me, civilization was usually Houston, Texas, but I discovered that there were plenty of trips away from Houston besides those to remote areas in the jungle and

How Jules Verne thought weightlessness would be. I had to fly to the Moon without my dog. (Bettmann / Getty Images)

Me at age six on Governors Island, New York, with Punch.

At Edwards Air Force Base during Test Pilot School with my F-104.

The Lockheed T-33, a two-seat version of the Shooting Star and the first jet I flew. (U.S. Air Force / Alejandro Pena)

My painting of the F-86 Sabrejet, our country's first supersonic fighter and the most enjoyable airplane I have ever flown.

Not much wing, but a big engine. The F-104 Starfighter, first fighter capable of flying at twice the speed of sound. (U.S. Air Force)

This is the type of airplane I first flew (when I was eleven)–a Grumman Widgeon. (U.S. Navy)

I learned to fly in a plane similar to this North American T-6. (Smithsonian Institution, National Air and Space Museum)

The Northrop T-38 Talon. We astronauts flew these regularly. (Michael Collins Collection, University Libraries, Virginia Tech)

Astronauts in training. *Top*: In Panama for tropical survival school. (NASA)
Bottom: Studying the rock formations in the Arizona Meteor Crater.

Charlie Bassett and me standing by our improvised desert home. (NASA)

Gliding across the "slippery table" and controlling my progress by squirting jets of air out of the gun in my right hand. (Michael Collins Collection, University Libraries, Virginia Tech)

A view of "the Wheel." A very unpleasant way to spend an afternoon. (Art Melliar/NASA)

A few seconds of weightlessness aboard the zero-G airplane. (NASA)

All suited up and ready (I hope) to fly Gemini 10. (NASA)

John Young (right) and me sitting in Gemini 10. Cramped quarters, especially with the hatches closed. (NASA)

Gemini 10 departs. Shake, rattle, and roll! (NASA)

We get our first look at our Agena target vehicle . . .

. . . and closer yet.

We light the Agena's engine, and it kicks like a mule as we head for home. (NASA)

desert. For one thing, the various parts of the Gemini and Apollo spacecraft were manufactured in factories as far apart as New York and California, with places in between such as St. Louis, Missouri. We could learn a lot about these spacecraft by reading about them in our Houston offices, but beyond that there came a time when we had to see them actually being put together and talk to the people who were building them.

Spacecraft are assembled in special rooms called "white rooms" or "clean rooms." They are special because everyone tries very hard not to allow even one speck of dirt to enter the room. The air is carefully filtered so that it is free of dust, and every item of equipment must be carefully cleaned before it is allowed to enter. The reason for these precautions is that the machinery inside a spacecraft must work perfectly. Some of it is very delicate, and even something as small as a human hair might get stuck in the wrong place and cause a computer to give a wrong answer. The most difficult part of keeping a "white room" really clean is people, who are always dirty—even just after a bath. They have mud on their shoes, and lint on their clothes, and their hair falls out without their even knowing it. The "white room" must be protected from dirty people, yet it is full of people working on the space-craft. The solution is to wrap them: their shoes are wrapped in plastic booties, their bodies in white nylon lint-free jumpsuits, their hair in nylon caps, and their hands in gloves.

Wrapped up like mummies, we new astronauts were given our first peek at the Gemini spacecraft being built at the McDonnell plant in St. Louis. I was amazed at the care and attention given each machine. I had thought it took a lot of care to assemble an aircraft, but they were just thrown together compared to the meticulous work being done inside the "white room" at St. Louis. It was also very helpful to see the spacecraft in various stages of assembly, so that interior parts were visible. Seeing and touching the actual machinery made it easier to understand what all these complicated parts did, instead of just reading about them in books. We also talked to the engineers who had designed the spacecraft, and exchanged ideas with them for improvements. We found out, too, that we astronauts were considered celebrities, and the workers at the factory wanted to meet us, and wanted us to sign things. The favorite thing to sign was a dollar bill. I don't know what people did with them (I guess they saved them instead of spending them), but I was always a little embarrassed when anyone asked for my signature. I was especially embarrassed to sign a dollar bill that had already been signed by John Glenn or one of the other five astronauts who had actually flown in space. I thought a lot about the Russian system, which only considers people to be cosmonauts *after* they have made a space flight, not before. That made sense to me.

Of course, it was not only people in factories who wanted to see astronauts, but also a lot of other people around the country. NASA thought it was a good idea for people to know more about our space programs, and so we astronauts were sent out to make speeches and explain what Gemini and Apollo were all about, and to answer questions. That is called public relations. Usually we were sent out for a week at a time, to visit half a dozen cities, making a couple of speeches a day as we went. It was really tiring work. I never guessed that just meeting people and talking to them could be tiring, but it really was. At the end of my first week, I was ready to go back to test flying—it was relaxing compared to speechmaking. And the questions. Over and over again, I got, How do you go poop and pee in space (not exactly the same way you do on Earth), What will your wife be thinking about while you are in space (I don't know), Why did you want to become an astronaut (because I didn't know I would have to make all these speeches).

At least there was one good thing about a speechmaking trip, just like the other trips we took. That was the T-38 jet trainer we flew. Instead of having to wait until there was an airliner going our way, we could set our own schedules by flying our own planes, and save a lot of time. We could also keep our brains and bodies accustomed to the rolls and turns of flight, although weightless space flight might feel different from flight in the atmosphere. The T-38 is a beautiful airplane; sleek and slim, it looks as if it is going 400 miles an hour when it is parked on the ramp. Its top speed is around 800 miles per hour. It is also a delight to fly. It has powerful hydraulic pistons hooked to rudder, ailerons, and elevator, which means that if you move your hand on the stick or your feet on the rudders ever so slightly, the airplane reacts immediately. For example, it is possible to do a 360° aileron roll in one second. By that I mean that during one second's time, by effortlessly moving your right hand a couple of inches, you can make the sky go from above you to below, to above again, while the Earth is going from down to up to down. If you practice a lot, you can learn to make this roll smoothly, so that the nose moves evenly and stops at exactly the same point it began, with the wings precisely level once again. You can also do loops, but they are not as much fun as rolls, because they take a lot longer. You can also play tag with the cumulus clouds, climbing and diving around and through them. With an airplane like a T-38 you can do things you never dreamed of, high in the quiet sky. During World War II, there was an American fighter pilot who was killed flying a Spitfire at the age of nineteen. His name was John Gillespie Magee, Jr., and he wrote a poem called "High Flight." It says, far better than I can, what flying is all about:

> Oh! I have slipped the surly bonds of Earth
> And danced the skies on laughter-silvered wings;
> Sunward I've climbed, and joined the tumbling mirth
> Of sun-split clouds—and done a hundred things
> You have not dreamed of—wheeled and soared and swung
> High in the sunlit silence. Hov'ring there,
> I've chased the shouting wind along, and flung
> My eager craft through footless halls of air. . . .

Up, up the long, delirious, burning blue
I've topped the windswept heights with easy grace
Where never lark, or even eagle flew—
And, while with silent, lifting mind I've trod
The high untrespassed sanctity of space,
Put out my hand, and touched the face of God.

5

Our group of fourteen astronauts, having successfully finished our jungle, desert, and classroom training, were now put to work. Al Shepard, the chief of the astronaut office, assigned each one of us a specific area of responsibility, in which we were to train ourselves to become experts. Buzz Aldrin was assigned mission planning, which meant he attended all the meetings on that subject. In 1964, we were trying to figure out how many flights in Earth orbit we would need to make sure that we were ready to fly to the Moon, and Buzz became our expert in planning these flights. His biggest problem was to calculate how many different kinds of rendezvous we had to practice before trying a lunar landing. Once two men were on the Moon, they could get back to Earth only by making a successful rendezvous with their third partner waiting in orbit.

Bill Anders was assigned the environmental-control system, which is a fancy name for all the plumbing on board a spacecraft. Some pipes carry oxygen to breathe; others carry water to drink or to cool equipment. Then there are a lot of fans and pumps and storage tanks and other things that Bill had to understand. For example, he knew that a spacecraft flying between the Earth and Moon would be in constant daylight ("night" simply means that the Earth is between us and the Sun, making it dark where we are). Bill learned that if a spacecraft were held steady in this region, the side pointed toward the Sun would get too hot, and the side in the shadow would get too cold. Therefore, the spacecraft had to be rotated, like a chicken on a barbecue spit, to distribute the heat from the Sun evenly on all sides of it.

Charlie Bassett's specialty was the simulators. Simulators are make-believe spacecraft in which the crew practices and learns to fly the real ones. They are most important, because without them the astronauts would make all kinds of mistakes the first time they got into a real spacecraft. Practice makes perfect, according to an old saying. I certainly don't think I ever got perfect, but I know I wouldn't have dared fly a real spacecraft without hundreds of hours of practice in a simulator. You can crash over and over again in a simulator without getting hurt, but your first crash in a spacecraft would be your last one.

Al Bean studied recovery systems, which means he had to learn all about the parachutes that lower the spacecraft gently into the ocean, and how the Navy frogmen would bring a raft alongside so that the crew could get out and into a helicopter, and how the spacecraft would then be hoisted aboard the aircraft carrier. Al Bean was a Navy pilot who had landed an airplane on a carrier many times, even at night and in bad weather.

Gene Cernan's area of responsibility was propulsion, which means knowing about all the rocket engines a spacecraft carries. On Apollo, the lunar module has one rocket engine that slows it down enough to land gently on the Moon, and a second one that boosts it back up into orbit. There are also a whole bunch of small rocket motors mounted in pairs around the outside of the spacecraft. These are fired briefly whenever the astronaut wants to change the direction in which the spacecraft is pointed.

Roger Chaffee's job was to learn the communications system—that is, all the radios and antennas on the spacecraft and on the ground. The three most important tracking stations on Earth were located in Spain, Australia, and California. If you hold a small Earth globe in your hands, you will see that, no matter which way you turn it, you will always be able to see one of Spain, Australia, or California. The idea was that as the Earth turned on its axis, an astronaut on the Moon would always be able to talk to Houston, if the radio waves were relayed through one of these tracking stations, depending on which one was pointed toward the Moon at that particular time. Roger also had to learn about all the radios on board the spacecraft, because it was very important that we be able to talk back and forth between the two Apollo spacecraft, as well as with the people on the ground.

Walt Cunningham studied the electrical systems, which were very complicated. Our spacecraft got its electricity from two sources: batteries and fuel cells. Batteries are familiar objects, found in automobiles and flashlights, but fuel cells were rare, and we didn't know much about them at first. In high-school science classes, the teacher sometimes shows how, if one passes an electric current through water (H_2O), the water can be separated into two gases: hydrogen (H) and oxygen (O). A fuel cell does just the opposite. It takes two parts of hydrogen (H_2) and one part of oxygen (O), puts them together, and gets water (H_2O) plus electricity. That is really neat, because the crew can drink the water and use the electricity to run machinery, and the whole system weighs a lot less than using batteries and a separate drinking supply. The hydrogen and oxygen are cooled on the ground until they become liquids, and then they are stored on board the spacecraft in insulated tanks—like giant thermos bottles. Oxygen must be really cold (*minus* 293 degrees) to change from a gas to a liquid, but that is warm as an August swimming pool compared to hydrogen's temperature as a liquid: minus 423 degrees!

Donn Eisele's specialty was the attitude and translation controls, and they are difficult to explain. Basically, the attitude controller on a spacecraft is like the stick on an airplane, and the translation controller is like an airplane's throttle. But it's more complicated than that. A throttle can just make an airplane go fast or slow in the same direction, but the translation controller, a handle sticking out of the instrument panel, can make a spacecraft change speed in any direction: up-down and left-right, as well as straight ahead. You hold this handle in your left hand and push it in whichever direction you want to go. As long as you hold it in that direction, the proper rocket motors will fire to cause the spacecraft to move in that direction.

The attitude controller looks like the end of a pilot's stick, and you hold it in your right hand just as you would in an airplane. It controls which way you are pointed. Just as in an airplane, if your nose is too far below the horizon, you pull the stick back, and vice versa. Same for keeping level with the horizon, by moving the stick left or right. But an airplane has rudder pedals also, and a spacecraft does not. The attitude controller can be twisted clockwise to move the nose right, and counterclockwise to make it go to the left, just like kicking the right or left rudder.

With your left hand on the translation controller and your right on the attitude controller, you are ready to fly the spacecraft. Pretend that you are the pilot of an Apollo command module and you wish to dock with the lunar module. First find it, and move your right hand until it is exactly centered in your window. Then, using your left hand, thrust toward it until you are approaching at the proper rate, and holding the correct alignment with your right hand, use your left to reduce speed and bring your nose gently into its docking ring. Simple, isn't it? I hope you didn't hit it too hard.

Ted Freeman was the astronaut office's expert on boosters. Boosters are also called launch vehicles, or rockets, or missiles. I don't know which is the best name, but I usually call them boosters. The biggest one of all is the Saturn V, which we used to go to the Moon. The Saturn IB is a smaller version used for Apollo Earth orbital flights, and the Titan II, smaller yet, was used to put the Gemini into orbit. Yet, compared to Earth machines, even the puny Titan II is extraordinarily powerful, its two main engines each producing 215,000 pounds of thrust. If you gave your family car 215,000 pounds of thrust, it could accelerate from standing still to two hundred miles an hour in the length of a garage. And remember that the Titan II is a shrimp compared to the Saturn V. The Saturn V produces seven and a half *million* pounds of thrust. It gulps liquid propellants at the rate of 15 tons per second, which means that it could suck an average swimming pool dry in seven seconds. Ted Freeman's main worry was that one of these monster boosters might blow up and smash the spacecraft to smithereens.

Dick Gordon's job was cockpit integration. He had to make sure all the dials and instruments and switches in the cockpit were properly located, so that the astronaut had all the information he needed, at the right time and in the right place. During launch or reentry, acceleration forces can cause an outstretched hand to weigh six or eight times as much as normal, and any switches needed at those times should be located where they can be easily seen and grabbed.

Rusty Schweickart's assignment concerned the experiments that would be flown aboard Gemini and Apollo. Flying to the Moon was an experiment in itself, so not many experiments were carried on the early Apollo flights, but on Gemini we tried to carry as many experiments on board as we possibly could. A lot of these involved cameras, taking pictures of the Earth or Sun or stars. Others were medical experiments, like seeing how many pulls on a huge rubber band it took to cause your heartbeat to double its usual rate. One even involved shaving parts of your head, to which electrical sensors were stuck, so that your brain waves could be recorded while you slept. We astronauts thought that was a silly one. The most complicated experiment I tried was to measure the angles between various stars and the Earth's horizon, and from those angles to calculate where my spacecraft was, and how much we needed to change our orbit to rendezvous with an unmanned Agena rocket.

Dave Scott's job was guidance and navigation, which we called G&N for short. The Apollo G&N system kept track of where we were at all times. It measured our distance from Earth and our speed, and included an extremely accurate clock, so we would know when to make changes in our course. The G&N included a sextant, an instrument for looking at the stars and measuring their direction. We navigated using the stars and the horizon of either Earth or Moon. The G&N was the most complicated of all our systems, and Dave Scott had to be smart to understand it all. It also took a lot of hard work and study for the rest of us.

C. C. Williams's job was called range operations and crew safety. What that meant was that when a booster was launched from Cape Kennedy with men on board, there had to be complete agreement between the astronauts and the people on the ground. If an unmanned rocket started to veer off course, the range safety officer would simply push a button and cause the rocket to blow up in mid-air, before it could fall down on houses or schools. But with astronauts on board, we wanted to make sure that as much warning time as possible was given to the crew, so they could separate their spacecraft from the booster, and that the destruct button, as it was called, would not be pushed unless it was absolutely necessary.

The specialty area I was assigned was pressure suits and EVA. Pressure suits, or space suits as they are better known, are what astronauts wear in space, and EVA stands for extra-vehicular activity; that is, working outside the spacecraft. EVA in Earth orbit got called space walking, although it really isn't walking at all. It should be called something else, perhaps space floating or cord dangling, because we were always attached to the spacecraft by a safety line. I asked to be assigned to this work for a couple of reasons. First, I thought that learning about pressure suits would be fascinating work. Second, I thought that my math background was not as good as that of some of my fellow astronauts, and that I should avoid the very complicated areas like G&N.

What does a pressure suit do, and why do astronauts need them? The basic problem is that there is no air in space. It is a vacuum, which means that a person has nothing to breathe. Just as bad, there is no gas pressure pushing on his or her body, so fluids inside the body would turn to gas, blood would literally bubble, and the person would die. Therefore, a pressure suit must do exactly what its name implies: it must keep pressure on the body. The gas we used was oxygen, so that not only was the astronaut's body protected, but he could also breathe the oxygen. If the proper pressure and temperature of oxygen could be maintained at all times, then the astronaut would be set to venture outside his spacecraft.

Well . . . almost ready, anyway. There are still a couple of other problems to solve. One is that the suit must be thick enough to protect the astronaut from the searing heat of the Sun and the icy chill of space shadows. It must be strong enough to withstand the impact of a micrometeorite without losing pressure. It must be compact, light, and rugged. It must contain a communications system. Most difficult of all, it must be flexible and mobile.

Think about a bicycle inner tube: it's nice and soft and floppy until you pump it up, when it forms a fairly rigid circle. Then, of course, it has to be encased inside a tire and rim, which holds its shape and protects it from punctures. A pressure suit is built in approximately the same way. There is a bladder of thin, soft rubber that acts as the inner tube. Then there is a restraint layer, which holds the bladder in and conforms to the shape of the astronaut's body. Then there is an outer layer, to keep out meteorites and the Sun's heat. The problem is that, unlike a bicycle tire, which always remains round, a pressure suit must constantly change shape. As the astronaut bends, it must bend; twist as he or she twists; and in general act as a tough outer layer of skin. Now, it is easy to move inside a suit that is deflated, like a floppy inner tube, but it gets to be hard work when the suit is pumped up, or inflated. Then the suit becomes rigid, and it is difficult to bend at the waist or elbow or shoulder. The suit designer must be part engineer and part magician to invent a suit that is safe and protective without being cumbersome and rigid.

I enjoyed working with the engineers who were wrestling with these problems. It required a lot of traveling, because there were different kinds of suits and backpacks and chestpacks, and they were made not in Houston but in far-off places like Connecticut and California and Delaware and Massachusetts. Since I was the astronaut office's specialist, experimental pressure suits were made to my size, and I was required to wear them under various conditions to determine their comfort, reliability, and mobility. This work really kept me busy, hopping around the country from one meeting or test to another.

Some of the tests were fun, but others were just plain

hard work. Whenever we wanted to simulate weightlessness, we flew in the back end of a Boeing KC-135, which was just like the rear of a commercial jet liner, except that all the seats had been removed and the walls had been padded. The KC-135 pilot would dive down, gain speed, and abruptly pull into a steep climb. Then he would push over, following an arc shaped like a parabola, and for about twenty seconds we and the airplane would fall together, temporarily weightless. During this twenty-second period, we would hurry through our tests.

One of the most difficult was to try to get back inside the Gemini cockpit and close the hatch over your head. The Gemini was very small, and while weightless, I used to keep popping up out of the cockpit, like a cork out of a bottle. It took all my strength to bend that suit enough to wedge myself down in the seat so that there was enough clear space over my head to close the hatch. On a typical flight, we would stay up in the KC-135 and do forty or fifty parabolas.

The first few times I tried it, it was fun, especially if I didn't have to wear a pressure suit. Once, we even dressed a friend up in a Superman suit and took pictures of him holding two other men at arm's length and then throwing them up in the air. That was easy to do while all three were weightless. But after a while the KC-135 stopped being fun and became hard work. For one thing, it was usually quite hot inside the pressure suit, and after a couple of parabolas of strenuous work I would be breathing hard and sweating a lot. Sometimes I even got a little bit of claustrophobia, which is an awful feeling that you are trapped inside something and must get out. Of course, I *was* trapped inside the pressure suit; when I didn't feel I was getting enough cool air to breathe, I would get a little panicky and raise the visor on my helmet to get a whiff of fresh air. That worried me because, of course, in space you couldn't raise the visor without deflating the suit and dying.

Another problem in the KC-135 was that the parabolas, and the pullouts between parabolas, tended to make you sick. I never got really sick myself, but the sight of a lot of engineers and photographers getting sick was not pleasant. It caused me to get a very queasy feeling in the pit of my stomach. Finally it got so bad that if someone came up behind me on the ground and whispered "KC-135" in my ear, my stomach would do a double backflip with a reverse twist.

A second torture chamber, worse than the KC-135, was the centrifuge. It was used to simulate the acceleration our bodies would feel during launch and reentry, where the body "weighs" many times more than normal. Unlike its opposite condition, weightlessness, it is easy to simulate. The centrifuge, which we nicknamed "the Wheel," does it simply by swinging you around in a circle. The faster you turn, the greater the centrifugal force pushing you into your seat, and the heavier you feel. Our centrifuge had a huge electric motor and a fifty-foot arm with a simulated spacecraft on its end. Built into a circular room, and controlled by a computer, the arm could be made to turn at whatever speed was necessary to imitate the loads we would experience under various flight conditions. The worst case was the deceleration an astronaut would feel if his rocket engine quit before he reached orbit, causing him to plunge back down into the atmosphere.

We practiced, for brief instants, up to 15 Gs, which means that my 165-pound body would be pressed up against its seat with a force 15 times that of its weight, or a total of 2,475 pounds—over one ton! Fifteen Gs is not pleasant. In fact, I start feeling uncomfortable at about 8 Gs, with a pain developing in the center of my chest. At above 10 Gs, I have difficulty breathing. The problem is that it is easy to exhale, and to empty the lungs, but almost impossible to move the chest muscles to reinflate them. A new breathing technique is required, one in which the astronaut pants like a dog, and takes many short quick breaths "off the top" of his lungs, and never allows them to become completely deflated.

Another problem at high Gs is that your vision is affected, and darkness closes in from the edges toward the center of your field of view. It's called tunnel vision because, before you black out completely, for a while you seem to be looking down a tunnel and can see only those objects that are directly in front of you. Sometimes the forces on your body at high Gs cause tiny blood vessels to rupture, usually in your eyes, so the doctors examine you carefully after a ride on "the Wheel."

You feel the centrifuge for hours after you get off it, in a way that is totally unexpected: if you turn your head suddenly to the side, you feel quite dizzy. You also feel tired whether you turn your head or not. All in all, riding "the Wheel" is not a pleasant way to spend your days. I remember one time there was a competition between three different types of pressure suits, to see which one would be selected for the Apollo flights. All three were made to my dimensions, which meant that I was the only one who could test them on the KC-135 and "the Wheel." Lucky me!

6

In June 1965, I really did get lucky. I was the first of our group of fourteen to be assigned to a flight crew. It was only a backup crew, which meant that I wouldn't get to fly unless something happened to the prime crew, but I was really excited nonetheless.

The flight was Gemini 7, and the prime crew members were Frank Borman and Jim Lovell. The commander of the backup crew was Ed White, and I was to be his co-pilot. I had known Ed for many years, as we had been classmates at West Point. I also knew Frank Borman well, because he and I had sat at adjoining desks at the Test

Pilot School. I had only known Jim Lovell for a year or so. Fortunately, I enjoyed being around all three of them, and they were a good group with whom to work. Ed White was a very good athlete, and he liked to start the day by running a couple of miles and end it by playing handball or squash for an hour, followed by a sauna bath. A sauna isn't really a bath at all; our sauna at Cape Kennedy was a small room with wooden walls, floor, and ceiling. We sat naked on wooden benches while an electric heater, buried under a pile of stones, heated the dry room to very high temperatures. After ten minutes or so at 170°, I would be red as a boiled lobster, but feeling good—relaxed, drowsy, and healthy. Often I needed the sauna to relax, because I was giving my brain a real workout. Frank, Jim, and Ed knew the Gemini spacecraft well, having spent months studying it while I was doing my pressure-suit work. Therefore, I had a lot of catching up to do. Gemini 7 was due to launch in a few months, and I had to be ready to fly it in case anything happened to Jim Lovell.

Ed White was a big help in explaining things to me. He had already flown in space once, aboard Gemini 4, and was our nation's first space walker. His EVA had lasted only about twenty minutes, but he had enjoyed it so much that he hated to get back inside the spacecraft and close the hatch. When he did, he found the hatch was stuck, and he had a difficult time closing it. Luckily, Ed was probably the strongest of all the astronauts; I don't think some of the others would have been able to close it. But that was something we didn't have to worry about on Gemini 7; there would be no EVA on this flight. It was a long-duration flight, and Frank and Jim were scheduled to stay up for two weeks, provided no machinery broke, and provided they seemed to be continuing in good health.

The idea behind Gemini 7 was that it would take more than a week for an Apollo spacecraft to fly to the Moon and back. No one knew what might happen to human beings who were weightless for that length of time, but we did know that if they became sick on the Moon, that was bad, since it would take them at least three days to get home again. So the thought was to test people for longer than an Apollo flight, but to do it in Earth orbit, where they could return to the ground quickly if necessary. Hence fourteen days for Frank and Jim; I thought that was really a very long time to spend inside the tiny Gemini cockpit. They would have more room sitting in the front seat of a Volkswagen. And their cramped

Gemini cockpit was all they had; they couldn't escape it. It was their office, study, living room, dining room, kitchen, bedroom, bathroom, and laboratory—all in one. Frank and Jim would really get to know each other as they circled the Earth more than two hundred times, eating, sleeping, going to the bathroom, working—all within inches of each other.

I found that I couldn't sit in the Gemini simulator for more than three hours before my back got sore and my legs became numb. Then how in the world were Frank and Jim supposed to stand it for two whole weeks? The secret was weightlessness. There would be no gravity to squash their bodies against their seats. Instead, they would float free, unless they chose to remain strapped down. Therefore, their backs shouldn't get sore or their legs numb—but I still think that is an awfully long time for two people to be locked up inside such a small enclosure. I am five feet ten inches tall. Inside a Gemini, I could touch my head against the hatch and my feet against the floorboards at the same time, without having to stretch. Sitting in the right-side seat, I could easily reach over and touch the left wall.

Weightlessness might be good for the body in terms of comfort, but it is thought to be harmful to the heart, muscles, and skeleton. The reason is that the body does not have to fight against gravity, and therefore becomes weakened. For example, a lot of the heart's work comes from the fact that gravity tends to cause the blood to pool in the lower part of the body, and the heart has to pump it "uphill" against the pull of gravity. In space, with no gravity, there is no "up" or "down" for the heart, and when it pumps, it has an easier job, having only to overcome the resistance of the veins and arteries. The muscles of the body also find their job easier, especially the leg muscles, which no longer have to hold a heavy body "up." In similar fashion, the skeleton finds it doesn't have to support any weight. When parts of the body aren't used, they tend to weaken, or shrink, or atrophy. The heart in space gets lazy, skeletal muscles decrease in size, and bones lose some of their calcium. In 1965, no one knew how bad these effects might be after two weeks in space, and it was Frank and Jim's job to find out.

Much later, in 1973 and 1974, Project *Skylab* kept astronauts in orbit for as long as eighty-four days, without harming them. The *Skylab* astronauts found that exercise was very important in keeping their bodies strong, and they liked to exercise for at least an hour a day. Of course, *Skylab* was a huge spacecraft and it was easy to exercise by riding a bicycle bolted to the floor, or by running around and around the walls. But in the tiny Gemini that was not possible; about all Frank and Jim could do was pull on a heavy elastic cord. They could loop it around their feet and then pull up with their arms and shoulders, stretching it as far as they could. In 1965, people weren't sure whether pulling on a rubber cord was going to help the heart any or not; in fact, even the astronauts weren't in agreement on the importance of physical conditioning. Some astronauts thought that since a trip into space would cause their hearts to get lazy, perhaps they should relax beforehand and not get much exercise. Others thought that if their bodies were going to weaken in space, they should start out as strong as possible, and that meant exercise.

I agreed with that idea, although I didn't think that I needed to spend hours a day exercising. It wasn't at all like being a professional athlete. It was just that the body should be healthy and lean, and the heart muscle should be strong. There are various ways of increasing your body's endurance, and they all involve putting a steady and sustained load on the heart muscle. Swimming and riding a bicycle for long distances are two good examples. Another is jogging, or running, and that is the method I prefer. The experts recommend a vigorous twenty-five-minute workout three times a week. Personally, I find that if I run two miles at a time, four mornings a week, then the doctors who give me physical exams say that I am keeping my heart muscle in good condition. Since this amount of running only takes an hour or so a week, I think that it is time very well spent. I notice that if I don't do it, I don't feel as well, and I tend to get tired more easily.

Another important factor in physical conditioning is smoking. Smoking is really bad. It is about the most stupid habit known to humankind. It causes lung cancer and other diseases, and it decreases the endurance of the heart and lungs. It's not that much fun either. I used to smoke a lot, for years and years, and I got to the point that I didn't really enjoy it at all, but I couldn't think about much else if I didn't have a cigarette every half hour or so. I was addicted to it. Since I stopped smoking, I feel much better, and I don't have to worry about setting my bed on fire (yes, I did that one time). Best of all, I know I am doing my body a big favor.

The effects of smoking on the body are now well-known, but the effects of space flight were largely unknown in 1965. We knew that the body has its own internal "clock" that tells it when to become tired and when to wake up. Called the circadian rhythm, this clock is geared to the place where you have been living recently. If you live in Houston and take a trip to the other side of the world, your body will want to go to sleep when it is late at night in Houston, even though it may be broad daylight where you are. In Earth orbit, it takes ninety minutes to go around once. During this hour and a half, the astronaut will see one sunrise, one noontime, one sunset, and one midnight. Does that mean he will get sleepy at dusk and wake up at dawn? No. His internal clock doesn't work that way. The body ignores the fact that its eyes are seeing a ninety-minute day-to-night cycle. It clings to the familiar twenty-four-hour cycle, so the astronaut becomes sleepy when it is his normal bedtime in Houston, regardless of what he sees out his window.

For this reason, we tried to program our activities in space for between 8:00 A.M. and midnight, Houston time. Of course, we couldn't always do that. Sometimes things take a certain length of time, and they cannot be sped up. For example, if you fly from the Earth to the Moon, it may just turn out that you arrive at the Moon at 4:00 A.M. Houston time, and you wouldn't want to be asleep for that! On the early Gemini flights, we were worried about the machinery breaking, so we decided it would be a good idea for one of the two men to be awake at all times. Not only was this arrangement bad for the astronauts' circadian rhythms, but the astronaut who was on duty made enough noise as he went about his work to keep his partner awake. After a couple of days of this, the crew would really be tired. On Gemini 7, Frank Borman and Jim Lovell were going to change this procedure. They would schedule their work together. Then when their wristwatches told them it was bedtime in Houston, they would put thin metal plates over their two windows to block out the Sun, and both would go to sleep, trusting the spacecraft not to break during the time they were asleep.

Heart muscles and circadian rhythms were interesting things to know about, but they were not the *most* important things, as far as we astronauts were concerned. We were most concerned about understanding the spacecraft, which was a very complicated bundle of machinery— any part of which could break. If something went wrong, what could we do about it? We tried to be reasonable and consider only the most likely possible failures. Even doing that, we filled books full of procedures for coping with emergencies. Most of the time, if something failed, we could take our sweet time in fixing the problem, but not always. During descent, for example, if the Gemini's parachute did not come out when scheduled, the astronauts really had to hurry to try other ways to get the chute out or, failing that, to eject themselves.

I understood *that*. Once, I had had to eject from a burning airplane, and I knew that the procedures had to be memorized and be very clear in your mind. An ejection seat is simply the aluminum seat the pilot sits in, with a small rocket motor built into the back of it. When the airplane is about to crash or blow up, the pilot can fire the rocket, which blasts him—still strapped in his chair—free of the airplane. Of course, it's not all that simple. In the F-86 Sabrejet (which was the airplane from which I ejected), you first had to disconnect your oxygen hose and radio cord, then bend over and jettison the canopy. Bending over was important; otherwise, the canopy would hit you in the head as it departed the airplane. Once the canopy was gone, you had to sit upright with your head back against the seat and squeeze a trigger in the right arm of the seat to blast you out of there. Sitting up straight then was *very* important; otherwise, you might break your back when the seat fired. Then, as soon as you were free of the airplane, tumbling end over end, unable to see because of the wind blast in your eyes, you had to reach down and unbuckle the seat belt, kick away from the seat, and open your parachute by pulling a D-shaped ring on the left side of your chest. Getting rid of the seat was very important. If you did not, the parachute would probably not open. All these things had to be done swiftly and correctly the first time. The time in the F-86, everything went well. There was a muffled explosion, my cockpit started to fill up with smoke, and my wingman told me I was on fire. I ran through the ejection procedures, and everything worked as advertised, except that the ground rushed up so fast I wasn't prepared for it. My body was in the wrong position when I hit, and I tumbled over backward with all the grace of a bag of potatoes. Luckily, I landed in a farmer's soft plowed field and was not hurt.

In the space program, we prepared for such emergencies by "flying" simulators. Simulators are imitation spacecraft that are hooked up to computers. You sit inside the cockpit of the simulator, which looks exactly like the real spacecraft. The computer causes the dials and gauges to move just as they would if various things were happening to the real spacecraft. For example, if an oxygen tank sprang a leak, the oxygen pressure gauge in the simulator would decrease, giving you a clue as to what had gone wrong. The simulators came with instructors, who could direct the computer to imitate one problem after another until we got the hang of it. Frank, Jim, Ed, and I spent many long hours in the simulator during the fall of 1965, getting ready for the flight in December. By launch day, Frank and Jim were really good at "flying" the simulator, which meant they should be able to handle the real spacecraft with ease. Nothing would go wrong in flight, we hoped, but if it did, the simulator should have prepared them well to do the right thing in any emergency.

I was glad Jim Lovell stayed healthy and was able to fly Gemini 7, but at the same time I was sad that I was not able to fly it myself. It's just too bad that there was only one seat for the two of us. Frank and Jim had a very nice flight and stayed up the entire two weeks, just as planned. Fortunately, nothing serious broke, so all that practice in the simulator was not needed. The best part of it all was that the doctors couldn't find anything seriously wrong with them after the flight, so it looked as if one big obstacle had been removed from the pathway to the Moon. After the flight, Ed White was transferred to the Apollo program, but I was assigned as prime crew, with John Young, on Gemini 10. I was disappointed to part company with Ed, but I was pleased to be able to fly with John, whom I liked. Most of all, I was excited at the prospect of flying in space. I would gladly have flown with Ed, or John, or by myself, or with a kangaroo. I just wanted to fly.

7

The Gemini 10 flight was going to be a lot different from Gemini 7. It was only a three-day flight, but it was jam-packed with fascinating things to do. First of all, there would be two Agenas in orbit, waiting for us. An Agena is a slim fuel tank about thirty feet long, with a rocket engine sticking out of one end and a hole in the opposite end. John Young and I were to rendezvous and dock with the first Agena, fitting the Gemini's nose into the hole, and locking the two vehicles together. Then we would use the Agena's fuel and rocket power to boost us into a higher orbit, where we would find the second

Agena, which had been in orbit for four months. We would fly alongside the second Agena, and I would space walk over to it and bring back an experiment package from it. In the process of catching the second Agena, we were expected to set a world's altitude record of 475 miles. There were also a dozen other experiments to keep us very busy for the remainder of the three days. I thought it was a neat flight plan, especially the space-walk part. I was really looking forward to stepping out of a spacecraft traveling 18,000 miles an hour.

John and I had six months (from January to July of 1966) to get ready for the flight. John had already flown once before, with Gus Grissom on Gemini 3, and was very familiar with the Gemini spacecraft. And, of course, I had just come from the Gemini 7 backup crew. But neither of us was prepared for rendezvous or space walks, and both tasks could be very complicated. First we had to find our own Agena, which would be launched into a circular orbit a couple of hours before John and I were scheduled to launch. Usually, the experts on the ground would tell a Gemini crew which way to steer to find their Agena, but on this flight—as an experiment—we were supposed to figure it out ourselves. We were to do our own navigating by measuring the angle between various stars and the horizon. From this, and a lot of arithmetic, we could figure out how to change the size and shape of our orbit to reach our Agena. As usual, the simulator was our teacher, and we spent long hours "flying" around and around in orbit, trying to figure out where we were and what we needed to do to reach our imaginary Agena. I filled page after page with numbers. Sometimes the simulator said my numbers were correct and that we reached the Agena. At other times we either missed it altogether or used up too much fuel reaching it.

One thing the simulator couldn't do was teach me how to space walk. The only way to *really* learn that was to try it, although my old friend the zero G airplane was somewhat helpful. For twenty seconds at a time, I could practice opening the Gemini hatch, getting out, and "flying" or walking over to the side of a make-believe Agena built out of wood. On the wooden Agena was an exact copy of the experiment package I would find on the real Agena, and it was attached in the same way.

I wasn't too worried about being able to remove the package. What did concern me was how I was going to get from the Gemini over to the Agena. If John could fly close enough to it, I supposed that I could stand up carefully in the hatch and give a little push with each hand

and float over to it. But suppose I pushed a little harder with one hand than with the other? That would cause me to start turning sideways, and I might turn all the way around before I got to the Agena, and crash into it with my back. In my bulky pressurized space suit (remember all the problems with *them*?), I couldn't do much to prevent that, or even to see where I would go if I bounced off. To add to the problem, I was connected to the Gemini by a fifty-foot-long cord, which contained oxygen to breathe and a couple of wires so that I could talk on the radio with John or with the people on the ground. What happened if the cord looped around the Agena? There was nothing to prevent me and the Gemini and the Agena from getting wrapped up like a Christmas package, with no way for me or John to untie the knot. Agenas have a system for keeping themselves pointed in one direction. It works off batteries. The Agena we were to visit, which had been in space four months, would have dead batteries by the time we got there. That meant that, instead of pointing steadily in one direction, it was free to wander off its heading. It might even begin to tumble or to spin. What were we supposed to do then? Was it safe to approach if it was moving rapidly? If moving slowly? No person, and no simulator, could give us exact answers to these

87

questions. A lot would depend on what we thought once we got there.

I did have one device for helping me move over to the Agena. I called it the "gun," although it had a fancier name: the hand-held maneuvering unit. It looked sort of like a pistol, with a stubby handle that I held in my right hand. On the top of the handle there was a crossbar with a hole in each end. There was also a hole in the end of the handle. There were two triggers. The idea behind the gun was simple: if I held one trigger down, nitrogen gas would squirt out the two holes, or jets, in the crossbar. If I held the other trigger down, gas would squirt out through the jet in the handle, in a direction opposite that of the two jets. By pointing the gun in the right direction, and by squeezing the correct trigger, I could cause the nitrogen gas to exert a force that would move my body either forward or backward. In theory, then, if I stood up in the Gemini hatch, pointed the gun at the Agena, and squeezed the two-jet trigger, I should be able to propel myself toward the Agena. When I got going fast enough, I would let go of the trigger and coast. Then when I got close to the Agena I would squeeze the other trigger to slow down and avoid crashing into it. I practiced with the gun a lot and found that it did work, but it was very difficult to use.

In addition, there was a training device in Houston built especially for the gun. It was a metal floor about thirty feet square, surrounded by a rope. It looked like a boxing ring, but I called it the "slippery table," because the metal floor was built to be as slick as possible. On the floor was placed a machine that looked like a floor polisher with a circular base about a foot and a half in diameter. Tiny gas jets allowed compressed air to squirt out under this base, causing it to rise a fraction of an inch off the surface, so that the machine floated on a cushion of air. The astronaut would stand on the "floor polisher." If he pushed against the ropes, he would glide effortlessly across the thirty feet to the other side, since there was not enough friction to stop him (because of the air cushion). Now, instead of pushing, if he held the gun in his hand and squirted in the right direction, the same thing would happen. If he held the gun improperly, he would end up moving in the wrong direction, or would turn around and around and crash into the ropes. I used to practice during the week in the simulator and in the zero G airplane, but I saved Saturday morning for the "slippery table." Dressed up in my pressure suit, and holding the gun awkwardly in my right hand, I would practice for hours, crossing and recrossing the table until I could propel myself to the exact spot I wanted, without going too fast and without twisting around. There was only one catch. The "slippery table" was only telling me part of the story. My body could twist only left or right, whereas in space I could not only twist, I could roll from side to side, and even tumble head over heels. Also, in my training I always stayed on the surface of the table, but in space I could rise up or sink down. The arm motions required to prevent twisting were complicated enough, but would mastering them enable me to prevent twisting, rolling, and tumbling all at once? I didn't know, but I would find out soon enough. Our launch date was approaching rapidly.

Before we flew, however, our boss Deke Slayton gave John and me one extra job. We were to join him and a couple of other people for a week. Our job was to select a new group of astronauts. It seemed strange for me to be sitting *across* from the hot seat, and I felt sorry for the poor sweating candidates as we interviewed them. It hadn't been very long ago, I reminded myself, that I had been in their shoes. We had about thirty-five people to

interview, and we wanted to spend at least an hour deciding about each one, so that meant a week's work, sitting
in a chair, asking questions, listening to the answers, and
then discussing this candidate in comparison with the
others. Strangely enough, we had very few arguments.
There seemed to be four things that were most important
to us in considering a person.

1. How smart was he?
2. How well educated?
3. What jobs or experience had he had that would
be helpful to him as an astronaut?
4. How badly did he want to become an astronaut?

Notice that I have said "he," because there were no
women in the group, nor were there any people of color.
In thinking about that, it seems to me that there were
plenty of women and people of color who could get the
highest marks in categories 1 and 4, but in 1966, categories 2 and 3 tended to rule them out. There simply did not
seem to be aeronautical engineers and experienced test
pilots who were people of color or women. I am happy that
this is no longer the case. Obviously, an airplane has no
way of telling the gender or skin color of the person
flying it. But I only know that we were asked to choose

among a group of thirty-five white males, and we did the best job we could. We ended up picking nineteen, and then John and I went back to preparing to fly Gemini 10.

As our July 18 deadline approached, John and I became busier and busier. When I was assigned to this crew, I had gotten into the habit of carrying a little black notebook around with me everywhere I went. The other thing I carried was a tennis ball. The tennis ball I used to strengthen my right hand, by squeezing it constantly. In this way I hoped that my right hand would not become tired during my space walk, when I would be required to squeeze the handle of the "gun" constantly, through the bulky pressure-suit glove. I used the black notebook to jot down each and every problem I found with the spacecraft or the flight plan. There was a total of 138 problems in my black book; as each one got solved, I drew a line through it. I hoped that before July 18 I could draw a line through the last one and go fly with a relaxed mind. In the meantime, if you came across someone looking worried with a black notebook in one hand and a tennis ball in the other, chances are that was an astronaut—a rookie astronaut, that is.

As July 18 came closer and closer, I did cross off every item on my list of 138. I also moved from Houston to

Cape Kennedy and visited my family only on weekends. Saturday I would practice on the "slippery table"; Sunday I saved for my family. Kate was seven years old and Ann was four. Ann was really too young to understand what was about to happen, but Kate understood quite a bit about the flight. I think she liked the idea, and I don't think she was worried. My wife *was* worried. I was sort of worried too, but I really wasn't afraid. I get afraid when I see the acrobats at a circus, sailing from bar to bar high above the ground, with no net to save them if they fall. I also get a terrible feeling in the pit of my stomach when I peek over the edge of a very high building. But like flying an airplane, the idea of flying in space did not arouse this kind of fear—only a vague uneasiness that something might go wrong. I was concerned not only about my safety, but also that I might embarrass everyone by doing something wrong. There were so many things to do in those three days that surely I would do some of them wrong. I only hoped that they would be little things, not the really important ones.

I tried to relax on Sundays. That was the day I would cook fancy dishes like lamb curry and mess up the whole kitchen. I would also play with our dog, Dubhe. This is the name of one of the stars in the Big Dipper, in the northern part of the sky. It is an Arabic name and is pronounced "Dooby." He was a big black-and-gray German shepherd, and he loved to play with the garden hose. I would hold it and squirt out a thin stream of water, which I kept just in front of him as he ran around in circles. When he caught the stream, he would snap his jaws with a loud click. No matter how many times he did this, he always seemed surprised that he ended up with nothing in his mouth, and the unharmed stream was still out in front of him. Then I would turn the hose on him and get him very wet, which he liked on hot summer days. After one last July Sunday with my family, I was ready to get in my T-38 jet and fly down to the Cape, climb on board Gemini 10, and spend three days circling the Earth.

8

Getting dressed for a space flight takes a long time. First, medical sensors have to be attached to your body. These are thin disks about the size of a quarter, which are stuck on your chest with a special kind of glue and then covered by adhesive tape. There usually are four of them and they are connected by wires to little electronic boxes in pockets around your waist, from which one cord goes out through your pressure suit and hooks up to the spacecraft. These sensors tell the doctors on the ground about your heart. The information from the sensors can be shown on a television screen in the form of a line that jumps upward every time your heart beats. From this, the doctors can tell not only whether you are dead or alive but whether you are resting or working hard and whether there is something wrong with your heart. The line is called an electrocardiogram. Doctors, like scientists, love to give long names to things. If your chest is hairy, it takes even longer to get the electrocardiogram machine all hooked up, because first someone has to shave little patches bare.

After the sensors are all attached, you put on long white cotton underwear and then crawl into your pressure suit, which is not an easy thing to do. You put your feet in first, through a zipper in the back of the suit, and then bend over double. Ducking your head, you put your arms through the same zipper opening and through the arms of the suit. Then your head pops up through the neck ring. If you have managed to push your arms and legs as far as they can go, then you will be able to stand up, just barely, and get someone to zip the back closed. By this time, you have begun to sweat, so you are hooked up through two hoses to an air-conditioning unit. Then you are ready to put on gloves and helmet, which are locked into place by metal rings that fit together. As soon as this happens, you are practically isolated from the rest of the world. You can hear only what is piped in over the radio;

you can breathe only 100 percent oxygen, which is usually odorless; you can't feel much through the gloves. The only sense that is unimpaired is sight. You can see the world fine, even if, locked up inside your pressure suit, you really don't feel you are part of it.

On the afternoon of July 18, 1966, John Young and I had gone through all this bother of suiting up and were ready to go fly Gemini 10. The reason for launching late in the day was that the old Agena, which had been in orbit for four months, would not pass overhead until then, and we wanted to launch when we were precisely underneath it, so it would be easier to catch. We rode out to the launchpad in a small van, and then took an elevator up the side of the gantry to the spacecraft, which was perched up on the nose of the Titan rocket. The elevator was not much more than a wire cage, and as it slowly ascended, I could see the beautiful blue Atlantic Ocean just a stone's throw away. It was quite a contrast, to see a huge pile of complicated machinery on one side and nothing but blue water on the other. Then it was time to crawl aboard our Gemini, feetfirst, with people shoving us down far enough in our seats so that our heads would clear the hatches. Once the hatches were closed and locked, John and I were in our own little world far, far away from the blue ocean and our friends and families. We were lying on our backs with our feet up in the air, and in a few minutes we would be lying on our right sides, one hundred miles up, going 18,000 miles per hour. I'm not sure I quite believed that, but I didn't have long to wait to find out, because now the voice on the radio was counting backward from ten.

Seven, six, five, four, three, two, one! We were off, not with a huge bang but with a small bump, as we felt the rocket come alive and begin to fly. It was noisy inside, but we *felt* what was happening, more than we heard it. Down below us, the two powerful Titan engines were churning away. They were also swiveling back and forth, keeping us pointed straight up, and it was this motion we felt as we jiggled slightly in our seats. There was no feeling of speed until we reached a thin deck of clouds. I could see them approaching, and then all of a sudden— *pow!*—we were through them, and I could tell that we were really moving. As we approached the speed of sound, the noise and vibration increased briefly, then things smoothed down considerably as we became supersonic. As the first-stage fuel tanks emptied, the G forces increased and pushed us back into our contoured seats at five times our normal weight.

When the second stage, or upper half, of the Titan separated from the first stage, I thought we had blown up. For a fraction of a second the view out my window changed abruptly. Black sky turned instantly to fiery yellow and I could see bits and pieces of something streaking past the window. However, as quickly as it had disappeared, the serene black sky reappeared, and I stopped worrying and began to enjoy the ride. As we approached orbit, the G forces built up past 7, and I felt a heavy hand pushing down on my chest. Then, suddenly, the engine cut off, the Gs went to zero, and we knew we had arrived.

Being weightless didn't feel too strange. I remained strapped in my seat, so about the only difference I noted was a feeling of fullness in my head, and my arms floated up in front of my face, like the front legs of a praying mantis. Also, of course, there was no force pushing me down into my seat, and my body bobbed against the shoulder straps and seat belt as I moved. There was no doubt that we were weightless, however, as the cockpit suddenly filled with tiny bits of debris that had come out of their crevices. There were small nuts and bolts, and screws, and fragments of metal and rubber. They floated aimlessly, until one by one they were slowly sucked into the intake screen of our air-conditioning system.

Outside my window the view was spectacular—a glorious vision of sea and sky I will never forget. Unfortunately, I didn't have any time to relax and enjoy it, because the spacecraft then plunged abruptly into darkness and I had to begin measuring star angles with my sextant, and doing the math to figure out where we wanted to go to find our first Agena. It took me a couple of hours to do this, and I really had a difficult time. I could see the stars all right in the dark, but it was next to impossible to find the horizon at night. There was no clear-cut line between black sky and black Earth. At any rate, when I compared my answers (expressed in terms of when and how much we should change our speed and direction) with the ground's answers, the two were different. I had flunked my first space test, and even though it was not a vital one, I felt bad about it.

Using the ground's instructions and our own rocket engines, we changed orbit several times and slowly approached our Agena. Finally, slightly over five hours after liftoff, John docked with it, smoothly moving the nose of the Gemini into the Agena's docking collar. The only problem was that we had used too much fuel in finding it, and that meant we might have to cut short some of our plans for the next two days. I hoped not.

Our next job was to find the second Agena, high above us. To change our orbit this time, we used the rocket engine on the far end of the docked Agena. That meant the rocket was on our nose, instead of behind us as usual, and its thrust would push us forward against the instrument panel instead of back into our seats. When the time came, I sent instructions to the Agena by pressing buttons on a small black box, and the Agena responded by lighting its engine. Boy, was that a surprise! First I thought nothing was going to happen, because I could see big blobs of fuel coming out of the engine and disappearing in the distance, like a string of snowballs. Then suddenly—WHAM!—the engine started, kicking like a mule and plastering us up against our shoulder straps. The whole sky turned a light orange color for the fourteen seconds the engine was scheduled to fire. Then another jerk, and we were weightless again. For half a minute afterward, the sky was filled with sparks, fireballs, and globs of fuel. Some seemed as small as fireflies, others as large as basketballs. Some particles floated off slowly, others whizzed away at a great rate. The entire Agena seemed surrounded with a golden halo that slowly faded into the blackness of space. "That was really something!" exclaimed John, and I agreed with him. "When that baby lights, there's no doubt about it." We were now in a slow climb up to 475 miles, and we had a chance to grab our first meal and some sleep.

I didn't sleep too well that night, for a couple of reasons. For one thing, astronauts usually find they are too keyed up by the events of launch day to really relax the first night. Also, it was strange sleeping in a cockpit instead of a bed. My hands kept floating up in front of me, and I wished I had pockets or *somewhere* to put them to keep them out of the way of all the switches on the instrument panel. I didn't want to bump the wrong switch accidentally while I slept. Maybe I should have stuffed my hands in my mouth. Also, my head didn't feel right somehow with no pillow to push against.

Finally, I found a little corner up above my head, to the right, and I discovered that if I wedged my head up into it, it felt more natural. I ignored my floating hands, and dozed off fitfully for a couple of hours. I needed to get as much rest as possible, since the next day was to be a busy one, and included my standing up in the open hatch and photographing a number of stars. Any time we dumped our cabin pressure and opened the hatch to the vacuum of space, we had to be extremely careful, and I didn't want to increase the chances of my making a mistake just because I was tired.

When the time came to open the hatch, everything worked beautifully. I opened it at dusk, and it moved easily in my hand, with no hint of binding. I stood up then, in the dark, and got my first good look at the universe all around me. Inside the Gemini, the view was limited by the tiny windows, and even more if you had an Agena stuck on your nose, but now I was able to look up and down and left and right. Stars were everywhere: above me on all sides, even below me somewhat, down next to that murky horizon. The stars were bright, with none of the twinkle we normally see on Earth. The twinkle is caused by the starlight having to penetrate the atmosphere, which moves and shifts, but up here above the atmosphere the stars burn steadily and brightly. The Moon was not in view, and the surface of the Earth was barely discernible. Occasionally there was a flash of lightning below us that illuminated a string of thunderstorms. There was a stately and graceful feeling of motion as we glided across the world in total silence and with absolute smoothness.

My job was to photograph half a dozen stars, which

had been chosen because they were young and were giving off a lot of ultraviolet light. I held the camera shutter open for twenty seconds for each star. John, inside the spacecraft, counted the seconds for me.

As dawn approached, we finished up this work and prepared for our next experiment. The Sun came up, as it always does in space, with a fierce burst of piercing white light. When it did, my eyes began to water, despite the fact that I had pulled my head down inside my neck ring, like a turtle, to avoid its direct glare. My eyes were watering so badly that I couldn't see the camera I was holding clearly enough to change some settings on it. I handed it inside to John and asked him to help me. Then I got the shock of my life! John couldn't see either, as his eyes were watering as badly as mine. What a fine mess we had on our hands, with the hatch open and neither of us able to see.

I threw away into space some additional photographic equipment I was holding in my other hand and prepared to get back inside the spacecraft. I had practiced this so many times in the zero G airplane that it seemed very natural now. Fortunately, there were no straps or hoses dangling loose. The hatch slid smoothly shut, all the way shut, and I was able to lock it without a great deal of tugging. Then we found the switches necessary to begin filling up the cabin with oxygen. My eyes began clearing up, and I could see well again. John's eyes took longer, but within ten minutes he, too, was seeing clearly, and we discussed the problem between us. Shortly, we came within radio range of a ground station, and we told them what had happened.

None of us could figure out why we had been blinded. There were two possibilities that I mentioned to John. First, we were using a new kind of anti-fog chemical to wipe on the inside of our visors, and I thought it likely that the sunlight had somehow reacted with it and produced a gas that irritated the eyes. A second possibility was that some of the chemical called lithium hydroxide had gotten into our eyes. Lithium hydroxide was used to absorb the carbon dioxide in our exhaled breath. It was supposed to be sealed inside a can, but some might have leaked out and might have been blown into our suits by the oxygen fan. Of course, it might also have been something completely different, and time alone would tell. Meanwhile, if it was either of the problems I described, then time was on our side, and things should get better. At least, we had overnight to sort these problems out, to determine whether a space walk was possible the next day. This next space walk was not as simple as yesterday's hatch stand, but involved my sailing over to the old Agena while John flew in formation with it. It would certainly require all our eyes and brains to be successful. In the meantime, I had to sleep, to rest up for the next day's activities, and this time I didn't have any trouble. I was so tired from a poor night's sleep the day before that I immediately conked out, and the next thing I knew, our third day in space had begun and the people in Houston were calling us on the radio.

Our first job, after a hasty breakfast, was to find the old Agena, the one with the experiment package on it. We had been getting closer and closer to it over the past twenty-four hours, and finally we saw it, a tiny speck some twenty-five miles in front and slightly above us. It was time to free ourselves from the other Agena, the one on our nose, so we released it and said goodbye as it slowly sailed off into the distance. As we drew closer to the old Agena, it changed from a speck to a cylinder, and I could see that it was not tumbling or spinning, but appeared to be steady as a rock. Good news, because I didn't want to get my umbilical line tangled up with a spinning Agena! We reached it shortly before sunset, just as planned, and John turned on our searchlight. As soon as it became dark, he had the difficult job of flying next to the Agena, keeping it in the center of the pool of light. While he was doing that, I was thrashing around over in my seat, getting all the equipment together that I would need for my space walk. I hooked one end of the fifty-foot umbilical line to the Gemini's oxygen supply and the other end to a chestpack, which in turn was hooked by two hoses to my pressure suit. I also hooked up radio lines, and I got my "gun" out and ready for use. At this time, the gun was empty. It got its supply of nitrogen gas from a tank in the rear of the spacecraft, to which I had to attach still another hose, but of course for that I had to wait until I got outside. Neither John nor I had had any trouble with our eyes since the day before, so Mission Control told us it was okay to go outside at dawn. As the sun burst into view, I was sitting there waiting, with a whole lapful of equipment. The fifty-foot umbilical line was all wrapped up in a ball; but even so, it was a big package, nearly as big as a basketball, and the cockpit was really crowded.

I got the hatch open without difficulty, and popped out into the sunlight. I could see the Agena about ten feet in front of and above me, but my first job was to turn my back on it and go plug into my nitrogen supply. There were handrails to help me reach the valve, which I did easily. However, once I got there, I had a bit of trouble getting plugged in. The end of the hose from my gun had a metal collar on it that was supposed to clamp over the end of the valve coming out of the side of the spacecraft. First the collar had to be cocked, and then it would snap forward and lock into place when it was pushed up against the valve. The trouble was that if the two halves were not aligned exactly, it would snap forward but would not lock, and then it would have to be recocked—a two-handed operation. The first time I tried, I didn't have the proper alignment, and the collar snapped forward but did not lock. This meant that I had to float free of the spacecraft, letting go of the handrail as I used both hands to recock the collar. The second time, it worked, and I was really glad, because I could tell John was getting worried. As I thrashed around and banged up against the side of the spacecraft, John could feel it, and so could the Gemini's control system, which didn't like the swaying motion and reacted by firing thrusters to hold the Gemini steady. This process wasted fuel, and we were running short of that and wanted to save what was left to get back down into a lower orbit after we had finished with this Agena.

Back in the cockpit once more, this time with a loaded gun, I was ready to sail over to the Agena. However, John was keeping us so close to it (about ten feet) that I decided I didn't even need the gun, but could just shove away from the Gemini and float over to the Agena. That may sound strange when you consider that we were roaring along at 18,000 miles an hour, but the important thing to remember is that the Agena was traveling precisely as fast; it didn't really matter how fast we were going, provided we were both going at exactly the same speed. And John was doing that, adjusting the Gemini's speed and position to exactly match that of the Agena. The Agena appeared motionless to me, therefore, as I stood in the open right hatch of the Gemini, peering up at the Agena's docking collar, ten feet away at the most.

When I was ready, I said, "I'm going to leap for her, John," and he replied, "Take it easy, babe." I pushed away from the Gemini gently, hoping that my right and left hand had each exerted exactly the same pressure, so that I wouldn't twist sideways. I also held my breath until my feet cleared the cockpit. If they had snagged on something, I would have pitched head downward and gone tumbling end over end. Fortunately, nothing snagged me, and I floated out slowly in the right direction. It wasn't more than a few seconds before I bumped gently into the end of the Agena. When I did, I noticed that part of the docking apparatus, a metal ring, had come free and was dangling loosely. I didn't want to get snarled up in that. I grabbed the end of the Agena with both hands, but it was hard to hold on, because the end of the docking collar was tapered and slippery, and my pressurized gloves were awkward. I had landed on the opposite side of the Agena from the spot the experiment package was located, so I had to go hand over hand around to it. When I got there, I discovered I couldn't stop. My legs kept going as the motion of my body pulled first my right and then my left hand free of the Agena, and I tumbled off into space!

At first I couldn't see a thing except the pitch-black sky as I slowly cartwheeled away from the Agena, but then the Gemini swung around into view. I found that I was about fifteen or twenty feet from it, in front of and above it, looking down at John's window and my own open hatch. I must have been just out of John's view, because he asked where I was. I began to explain, as I looked around. The Agena was below me on my left, and a loop of my umbilical line was awfully close to it. My motion was taking me away from the Agena and off to one side of the Gemini. I decided it was time to use my "gun," to propel myself back to the Gemini. When I reached for it in its customary place on my hip, it was gone! I groped around until I found the hose leading to it, and discovered that the gun wasn't really gone; it was just trailing out behind me. I reeled in the hose, grabbed the gun, and started squirting nitrogen. My flight path carried me in a great sweeping arc around and behind the Gemini.

I finally got straightened out and was approaching my open hatch from the rear when John told me he was going to have to move the Gemini downward, to stay with the Agena. I told him, "Don't go down right now. *John, do not go down.*" If he went down, I might sail over the top of the Gemini and miss it entirely. Also, which might be even worse, going down meant that he would have to fire some thrusters pointed upward, and I would be coming in directly over them. No one knew what would happen if their very hot exhaust gases touched my suit. The suit might even melt, and I wasn't eager to find out. Anyway, John delayed long enough for me to reach the cockpit, banging into the open hatch and hanging on for dear life. Then he moved the Gemini back into position near the end of the Agena, and I decided to make another try for the experiment package. This time, instead of pushing off with my hands, I used my gun,

111

pointing it up at the Agena docking collar and squeezing the trigger.

I rose slowly in the cockpit. As my left boot reached the top of the instrument panel, it snagged briefly on something, and I began a slow face-down pitching motion. Just as a diver wants to hit the water headfirst, not flat on his back, so did I wish not to splat into the Agena back-first, so I had some quick work to do with the gun. After a bit of squirting, I got myself pointed in the right direction again, but in the process I found I was causing myself to rise up above the end of the Agena, which was fast approaching. As it went by, I was barely able to reach my left arm down and snag it. As my body swung around the end of it, I plunged my right hand down underneath the docking collar and found some wires to hang on to. I wasn't going to fall off an Agena ever again! Now I repeated my earlier hand-over-hand trip around the end of the Agena, heading for the experiment package. But this time I clung to wires all the way, and was able to stop my motion when I got there, rocking back and forth a few times before I got myself steadied. Again the loose piece of metal appeared to block my path, and John voiced his concern about it: "Don't get tangled up in that thing!" Fortunately, I didn't, and I was able to pull the experiment package free easily with one hand. Then it was time to get back to the Gemini. I decided not to use the gun, but simply to come in by pulling hand over hand on the umbilical. That was all right, provided I didn't get going too fast, because I had no way to slow down, and I didn't want to splat up against the side of the Gemini too violently. One gentle tug and I was on my way, although I didn't move in a straight line but swung in a great circle around the side and rear of the Gemini and eventually reached the cockpit and handed the experiment package in to John. Then I made a sad discovery. I had lost my camera. It had been attached to my chestpack but had worked its way loose and was now out there somewhere in its own orbit. A couple of times during my space walk I had slowed down long enough to take a picture or two, and I knew I had some great ones, but now they were gone forever.

Next on our schedule was a practice test of the gun, to see how accurately I could use it. The ground called up, however, and said we didn't have enough fuel left to do that, and for me to come back inside the Gemini and lock the hatch. As I stood in the open hatch, gathering up all fifty feet of the umbilical line, I had a brief moment to rest and to look around. I felt fine; the only part of me that felt tired was my fingers, which had gotten quite a workout inside those bulky pressurized gloves. I also realized with a start that the Earth was down there! I hadn't even noticed it during the time I had been outside, having been completely preoccupied with the Gemini and the Agena.

My problem now was the umbilical line. Fifty feet of heavy hose, containing oxygen tubes and radio wires, is quite a bundle. In addition to its bulk was the distressing awareness that several loops of it were wound around my body. With John pulling, and me backing out of the cockpit a couple of times, we got rid of all but one last persistent loop. This was something I had never practiced in the zero G airplane, the matter of getting snarled in the umbilical, and I didn't like to think about what it would mean when I tried to squeeze down far enough to get that hatch closed. I looked down inside the cockpit and could barely make out John's shoulder. Loops of umbilical were everywhere! Well, now was the time to find out. I wedged my body through the nearly solid sea of coils, forcing my legs deep into the cockpit and jackknifing my knees so that my upper body swung downward and inward. I grabbed the hatch above me and pulled it inward. I knew it was going to hit either the hatch frame or my helmet. If hatch frame, fine, but if helmet, that meant I wasn't down far enough, and I would have to go back outside and try again.

Which would it be? *Click!* The best sound ever, as the hatch slid smoothly into place. Now all I had to do was unstow the locking handle, and crank, and crank, until—finally—it was locked. Then I tried to be funny. "This place makes the snake house at the zoo look like a Sunday school picnic," I said, referring to the fact that I couldn't see much besides a jillion loops of umbilical line. John and I took a good fifteen minutes to get that umbilical and all the rest of the space-walk equipment under control. We put it all together into one large package, which we then dropped overboard, opening the hatch for the third time in two days. This time, with no umbilical, the inside of the Gemini seemed quite spacious, and it was really easy to squeeze down far enough to get the hatch locked for the final time.

After all this, it was time for a good meal and some sleep. It was suppertime, and I had missed lunch in the rush of preparing for the space walk, and I was really hungry. I unpacked a transparent plastic tube of powdered cream of chicken soup, and filled it up with water. The water came from a gray metal water pistol with a long skinny barrel, which I stuck into a small opening in one end of the bag. The water gun was the same one John and I drank from, being attached by a tube to a large water tank in the back of the spacecraft. Every time you pulled the trigger, it would squirt one half ounce of water into your mouth (or wherever it was pointed). Now I mushed up the soup by squeezing the tube until all the powder was dissolved, and cut off the end of the tube with a pair of scissors. I stuck the open end in my mouth and squeezed. Delicious! The best soup I had ever tasted, even if it wasn't very hot (our water was kind of cold). Also, out my window I had the most exciting view I had ever seen, so my stomach and my eyes were very happy. Having finished my cream of chicken soup, I munched on squeezed bacon cubes and watched the world go by.

To save fuel, we had turned off our control system, which meant that we were slowly tumbling. Having flown fighter airplanes for years, I was accustomed to rolling and looping and even spinning, but I had never flown sideways or backward before. Now the blunt snout of our Gemini was tracing graceful arcs in the sky, sometimes in front of our direction of travel, sometimes to one side or the other, sometimes behind. It was like a beautiful roller-coaster ride in slow motion, with no noise, no banging around, no hollow feeling in the pit of the stomach. It was really fun. We were supposed to be going to sleep shortly, and I was tired, but not sleepy, and I really wanted to take the time to enjoy what I saw and felt.

We were flying at an altitude of 200 miles above a sphere whose radius is 4,000 miles. In other words, we were skimming along just above the atmosphere, which is very thin, thinner proportionally than the rind on an orange. The curvature of the Earth was apparent, but it was not startling. We were moving at 18,000 miles an hour, but there was not the blur of speed that one sees from a race car. The reason for this is that our higher speed and higher altitude combined to make things go by the window at the same rate as if we had been going lower and slower. The colors were also familiar, although the sky was absolutely black instead of blue, and one noticed the blue of oceans and the white of clouds more clearly than the green of jungles or the brown of deserts. Well, then, what *was* so different, so unusual, that I felt I could spend weeks looking out my small window?

It was simply that I knew how different it was, from a lifetime of crawling around the surface of this planet. It gave me a feeling of power to know I was circling the Earth once each ninety minutes. Those weren't lakes going by the window—those were oceans! Look at that! We had just passed Hawaii and here came the California coast, visible from Alaska to Mexico, and my bacon cubes not yet finished. San Diego to Miami in nine minutes, and if you missed it, it didn't matter, because they would be back again in another ninety minutes. Another difference was that we were high above all weather, in pure unfiltered sunlight that cast a cheery glow on the scene below. It seemed like a better world in orbit than it did down on the surface. The Indian Ocean flashed incredible colors of emerald jade and opal in the shallow water surrounding the Maldive Islands, then on to the Burma coast and lush green jungle, followed by mountains and coastline. Then out past the island of Formosa, looking like a giant, well-fertilized gardenia leaf, and across the Pacific, over Hawaii, and now time for California once again. Incredible!

But all good things must come to an end, and now it really was time to sleep, so John and I put thin metal plates over our windows and blocked out the spectacular view. I slept well, being by now much more accustomed to my surroundings, and, besides, I was tired and pleased from my day of space walking.

After a hearty breakfast when we woke up, John and I

performed a couple of hours of experiments, and then it was time to come home. We did this by firing our retro-rockets, four solid-propellant rockets mounted in our tail. We were to point backward when we fired them, so that they slowed us down enough to allow gravity to bend our orbit back into the atmosphere. We were scheduled to fire our retro-rockets over the Pacific Ocean, west of Hawaii, whereupon we would begin a gradual descent and finally splash into the Atlantic Ocean east of Florida thirty minutes later.

Before we could retrofire, however, we had a long checklist to wade through. And did John and I take our sweet time! We could fire those rockets only once, and everything had better be right. If we fired them while we were pointed forward instead of backward, instead of reentering the atmosphere we would be boosted into a higher orbit, with no way to get down from it. So as we went around on our final orbit, we double-checked everything except the direction we were pointing. We checked that at least ten times. It was also traditional to use the last orbit to say goodbye to the people in the various tracking stations who had helped us. "We'll be standing by," they told us. "Have a good trip home." "Roger," said John. "Thank you very much. Enjoyed talking to you.

It's been a lot of fun . . . Want to thank everybody down there for all the hard work." John wasn't kidding. The people on the ground had really been helpful, especially in thinking up ways for us to save fuel after we had used so much in finding our first Agena.

Finally the moment arrived, and a voice from below counted us down: *five, four, three, two, one*, RETROFIRE! After nearly three days of weightlessness, I had forgotten what acceleration felt like, except for those brief bursts from the Agena. Now I counted the four rockets as they fired one after another, and they really felt powerful. I was pushed back in my couch with an acceleration of one half G, but it felt more like 3 Gs to my sensitized body. As we descended, John flew the spacecraft while I worked with the computer to figure out where we would come down. As we entered the upper atmosphere, there was a five-minute period in which we were "blacked out;" that is, we couldn't talk on the radio. This strange fact is caused by an electric charge that surrounds the spacecraft and in turn is caused by the great friction produced when the spacecraft hits the atmosphere at high speed. Our heat shield was forward and our heads were pointed down toward the Earth. John banked this way and that, depending on the steering information coming from our computer. It was like making gliding turns to an airport, except that we were coming in upside down and backward.

As I looked out behind us, I could see that we were developing a long tail. This was caused by little pieces of our heat shield burning up and coming off, as it was supposed to do, to protect us from the searing frictional heat. At first the tail was very thin, but then it became thicker and brighter, glowing red and yellow in the dark sky. It was very pretty. As our G level built up to 4, I really felt heavy, but it didn't last long, and then we were down below the greatest heat and deceleration, and it was time to try the parachutes. First out was the drogue, a small parachute (six feet across) designed to slow us down enough to open our main chute. When the drogue came out, we began to swing wildly and I got slightly nervous, but then things quieted down a bit, and at 10,000 feet we unfurled our main chute, nearly sixty feet in diameter. It inflated with a great *whap* and filled our windows with red and white nylon. Beautiful! Soon after the main chute deployed, we noticed a strange thing. In addition to coming straight down, we were turning sideways. Apparently we were spinning on the end of our parachute line, and I didn't like that a bit. I figured it would make us descend faster and we would hit the water like a ton of bricks. We didn't, though. We must have caught the edge of a descending wave, because there was a gentle splash, and then our windows were full of white foam and blue-green water.

The sea was quiet, which was really helpful. A spacecraft does not have a keel or a deep hull like a boat, and it bobs and weaves with even the slightest wind or waves. I did not want to get seasick. Outside, I could see one of our thrusters still smoking, and then a helicopter flashed by the window. Inside, it was hot, and I suddenly realized how dry and cool it had been for the past three days. Now that we were back on Earth, it was moist and smelled like burned chemicals, but mostly it was *hot*. I had my pressure suit half-filled with sweat by the time we got our hatch open and were out into a rubber raft, up into a helicopter, and back onto the deck of our aircraft carrier. The flight was over, and I was ready to get out of that pressure suit.

9

Now I was a real astronaut, not just a rookie who hoped to fly in space. John Young was off to Orlando, Florida, for a hometown parade, but I don't really have a home town, so after a brief vacation at the beach I was ready to start working on Apollo. I had thought that the Gemini spacecraft was pretty complicated, but it seemed like a toy compared with the Apollo equipment. There were two Apollo spacecraft—the command module and the lunar module. The command module was scheduled to fly first, and my initial job was to learn it. It was so complicated that I really felt stupid when I got inside it. There were so many pipes, valves, levers, knobs, brackets, dials, and handles—and I didn't have any idea what most of them did. Not to mention switches. In the command module, there were over *three hundred* of one type of switch alone. I was assigned to a crew with Frank Borman and Tom Stafford. Frank was the commander, Tom was the command-module pilot, and I was the lunar-module pilot (although we didn't have a lunar module yet). At that time we were the only crew with no rookies on it, and I thought we had a good chance to be the first men on the Moon. I liked that idea.

I also liked some of the training I was getting. For example, before anyone could fly a lunar module, they had to have several hundred hours of practice in a helicopter. We had a couple of small helicopters in Houston, and I enjoyed flying them. Today, modern helicopters are automated, but learning to fly our early models took some getting used to: it was sort of like rubbing your stomach with one hand while patting the top of your head with the other. Try it. In our training helicopters, both hands were busy all the time. Your left hand held a stick containing the engine throttle, plus the control that made the helicopter go up and down. If you wanted to go up, you pulled up with your left hand. This caused the rotor blades to twist slightly and grab a bigger bite of air, and up you went. At the same time, the blades tended to slow down, so you had to twist your left wrist to add throttle, to keep the blades turning at the same speed. While all this was going on, your right hand was holding a different stick, and your feet were on the rudder pedals. Your right hand could not let go, even for a second, or the helicopter would tilt out of control, up-down or left-right. The rudder pedals kept the nose pointed straight. You were busy, but after you got the hang of it, it was great fun—a lot more fun than rubbing your stomach while patting your head. Although these helicopters didn't fly very fast, in many ways I preferred flying them to flying a speedy jet, because you can slow down to zero and do more things with them.

The reason we had to practice in helicopters was that the lunar module's descent to the surface of the Moon was very similar to a helicopter's vertical descent and landing. In Houston, we even had an imitation lunar surface, a slag-covered field with make-believe craters in it. Slag looks like pieces of porous rock but actually is the cinders left over when iron ore is melted down to make steel. It was gray in color and when you flew over this field in your helicopter it looked just like the photographs of the Moon. As we glided in toward a landing in the early morning or late afternoon, we could judge how high we were by the shadows on the craters, just as we would on the Moon. Sometimes I also chased birds in the helicopter, but of course that was not part of our training. I did learn, however, that even the most awkward bird is a *much* better pilot than I.

In addition to flying the helicopter in Houston, I was spending a lot of time flying to and from Los Angeles, where the command module was being assembled. The one assigned to Borman, Stafford, and me was coming along nicely, and I was finally getting to feel at home in it and learn what all the switches did. At about this time, however, the whole series of planned Apollo flights was rearranged. In the process, Tom Stafford was assigned a crew of his own, and I took his place. Bill Anders took mine, making the new lineup Borman–Collins–Anders. The only problem with this rearrangement was a rule that said no rookie could stay in the command module by himself. It had to be someone who had flown in space before. That meant me, because Anders was a rookie, and that meant that I got "promoted" from lunar-module pilot to command-module pilot. From that day on, although I later changed crews, I never changed specialties. Today a lot of people ask me, On the Apollo 11 flight, how did you and Aldrin and Armstrong decide who was going to stay in the command module and who was going to walk on the Moon? I usually just mumble, because it is very difficult to explain all these rules and crew changes. At the time I was very sad, because that was the end of my helicopter flying and my bird chasing, and because I suspected that once I became a command-module specialist, I would never be anything else again. But, on the other hand, I was pleased to be on *any* crew, and Borman–Collins–Anders had a fascinating Earth-orbital flight planned, one that was supposed to take us up to 4,000 miles, far higher than anyone had ever ventured. From 4,000 miles, we would be able to see the *whole* Earth, from North Pole to South Pole, something no one had ever been able to do before.

In January of 1967, the first Apollo crew was about ready to fly. Gus Grissom had flown twice before, once aboard the Mercury Liberty Bell 7, and once aboard the first manned Gemini. Ed White, my old partner, had been our nation's first space walker. Roger Chaffee, who had been picked to be an astronaut in the same group as me, was a rookie—and the third man on the crew. The three of them were sealed up inside their Apollo command module on the launchpad at Cape Kennedy when a fire broke out inside the spacecraft. The atmosphere inside the spacecraft was 100 percent oxygen, instead of normal air, which is only 20 percent oxygen. The difference is that things burn much more rapidly in 100 percent oxygen, and within seconds the inside of their spacecraft was filled with smoke and flames. The three astronauts died almost instantly, without any chance of escaping. As soon as this tragic news reached Houston, our whole community was filled with a great sense of shock. For years we all had known that space flight was dangerous and could actually kill someone, but now it had happened—and on the ground, at that. What had gone wrong? What were we supposed to do now? Were Grissom, White, and Chaffee the only ones who would die, or just the first in a long series? Of course, no one knew the answer to the last question, but as several months went by, answers to the first two became apparent. Something had gone wrong in the electrical system of the command module, resulting in a short circuit. This, in turn, caused a spark, which caused some flammable material to burst into flames.

Three things had to be done. First, the electrical

systems of all future spacecraft had to be carefully checked for possible short circuits. Second, all highly flammable material inside the spacecraft had to be replaced. Third, 100 percent oxygen would not be used on the launchpad, at full atmospheric pressure, but would be used only in orbit, at one-third atmospheric pressure. These changes took a long time to make, and it was nearly two years after the deaths of Grissom, White, and Chaffee before the first manned Apollo finally flew.

It was especially difficult to find non-flammable materials to substitute what we already had. The pressure suits, for example, had been covered with nylon, and that was replaced with something called Beta cloth, which did not burn as easily. Beta cloth was woven from glass fibers. The only trouble with this change was that Beta cloth is also very fragile, and if your knees or elbows got even a little bit worn, the glass fibers would come loose. In the weightlessness of space, they would float around freely, and it was quite possible that an astronaut might inhale them. Once in his lungs, there was no way to get them out again, and they might cause permanent damage. A fireproof coating had to be developed, therefore, to put over the Beta cloth to prevent it from flaking off. Finally, Teflon was selected. Thus one problem created a second, which created a third. A string of complications like this seemed common in the space program—at least it did in 1967 and 1968.

Finally, Wally Schirra and Donn Eisele and Walt Cunningham got the first manned Apollo into the air. Called Apollo 7 (because there had been six unmanned tests before it), they stayed in Earth orbit for ten days. It was an amazingly successful flight, and cheered us all up, even though I suppose we all still thought a lot about the dreadful fire. Before we could land on the Moon, however, we still had a lot of work to do. Wally Schirra and his crew did not have a lunar module, because it was not yet ready to fly. Also, they were launched by the Saturn IB booster, which was the baby brother of the huge Saturn V required to reach the Moon. We astronauts worried about the development of the lunar module and the Saturn V. However, I think the one thing that concerned us most in planning future flights was bringing the command module and the lunar module together in orbit around the Moon.

If the lunar module took off from the surface of the Moon at exactly the right time and in exactly the right direction, it would be fairly simple to catch the command module as it whizzed by overhead. But if the lunar module had to take off early or late, or got into a lop-sided or crooked orbit, then all kinds of trouble could easily develop, and the rendezvous process could become very complicated indeed. If the lunar module had to take off late, it would be further behind the command module than usual, and would have to fly faster to catch up with it before its limited oxygen supply was all used up. In orbit, to fly faster you have to fly lower, so the further behind the lunar module was, the lower the orbit it would aim for.

That idea was fine right up to the point where the lunar module was just skimming the mountaintops (there being no atmosphere on the Moon, you can orbit right down to the surface; in Earth orbit, you have to stay up above the atmosphere, or nearly a hundred miles up). If the lunar module was so far behind the command module that even mountain skimming wasn't going to allow it to catch up fast enough, the command module could help a bit by going higher, and therefore slower. But if this was not of sufficient help, then a whole new game plan went into effect, and the command module and the lunar module switched roles. The lunar module, instead of trying to go low and fast and catch the command module, went as high and slow as possible, while the command module dove down and made a fast extra turn around the Moon and caught the lunar module from the rear. In other words, the command-module pilot could normally expect to be the target, the hunted one, but under some circumstances their role might swiftly be reversed, and they would become the hunter! The problem with all this was that their work inside the command module changed completely, depending on whether they were hunter or hunted, whether they had to go high or low.

And I have only described one situation, that of the lunar module taking off late. There were many other emergencies in which the lunar module might find itself, and the command-module pilot's job as rescuer was a very complex one. In some cases, they simply would not have enough fuel to change orbit enough to catch the lunar module. If that happened, the pilot was expected to leave the other two crew members in lunar orbit and come back to Earth by himself. I didn't like that idea one bit, but it made more sense than having the command-module pilot die unnecessarily.

My life was not all work and worry, however. One time in 1967 my wife, Patricia, and I got to go to Paris for a couple of days to see an air show and to meet two

Russian cosmonauts. I always like air shows. It is exciting to watch the airplanes looping and rolling over the runway at low altitude. It's the next best thing to flying yourself. And, of course, we had never met any cosmonauts, and we wondered what they would be like. I liked them, especially Colonel Pavel Belyaev. It was difficult to talk to him, as our interpreter did not know much about space flight and its special language, but Pavel seemed friendly, and his life as a cosmonaut seemed similar to mine as an astronaut. We shared some of the same ideas and likes and dislikes. For example, neither one of us cared much for the space doctors and the complicated medical equipment they made us carry on board our spacecraft.

I remember thinking that I would have enjoyed flying in space with Colonel Belyaev, despite the fact that our two countries were not friendly in 1967. It was not until much later, in the summer of 1975, that two Russian cosmonauts and three American astronauts finally did make a joint space flight, with an Apollo command module visiting a Russian Soyuz in Earth orbit. I think such flights are a good idea. It takes a lot of trust to put your life in someone else's hands, and that is what you do when you enter a strange spacecraft. If that sort of trust between two countries can exist for a space flight, why cannot it develop into friendship in other areas as well?

After our trip to Paris, I plunged into preparations for my own Apollo flight. One of the things I had to learn was the guidance and navigation system. We called it G&N for short, but there was really nothing short about it. It was the most complicated part of the spacecraft, and took the longest time to learn. It began with the stars. There are five or six thousand stars that can be seen with the naked eye. Thirty-seven of these had been picked, because of their brightness and location, for us to use in navigating. We had to learn all their names and memorize where they were in the sky, so that no matter which way we were pointed, we could always find a couple of them. Once we found them, we focused an instrument called a sextant on them, and measured their direction precisely. Then we told the computer which star we had picked by a number each had been assigned. Combining this information with what the computer already knew about our speed and so forth, we could fly to the Moon and back without help from the ground.

I enjoyed studying the stars. Mostly we used a planetarium rather than the real sky, because that way we didn't have clouds blocking our view, and also we could see *all* the stars (those in the Southern as well as the Northern Hemisphere) without traveling to different parts of the Earth. Arabs were among the first seafarers, and they navigated using the stars. Consequently, many of the stars today have Arabic names, which I think are beautiful too. Altair, Deneb, Vega. Enif, Fomalhaut, Nunki. Adhara, Mirzam, Menkar. Aldebaran, Mirfak, Thuban. I love those names, and I didn't mind memorizing where each one is in the sky. They are always there; they never change position; and they are very far distant.

The star closest to us is called Alpha Centauri, and it is over four light-years away. In other words, if we could travel at the speed of light (186,000 miles per second), it would take us over four years to reach the nearest star. According to Albert Einstein, the speed of light is the fastest it is possible to go, so if he is correct, we will never be able to visit any star (except our Sun, which is a star) unless we are willing to spend many years traveling.

It gives me a strange feeling to think about how big our universe is. For example, let's say you go out into your backyard on a clear night and find the star Betelgeuse (I pronounce it "Beetle Juice"). It is in the constellation Orion, which is easy to locate. Now point your flashlight at it. That light will eventually reach the star, but by the time it does, you will have been dead a long, long time. Perhaps your great-great-great-great-great-grandchild may be alive when your flashlight beam reaches Betelgeuse, and remember that there are stars much, much farther away than old Beetle Juice!

While I was struggling to learn Apollo, it seemed to me the most important thing in the whole world, but suddenly I discovered that it really wasn't. Something was wrong with me, and I realized my health was a whole lot more important to me than any spacecraft. I first noticed my problem when I was playing handball. My legs didn't seem to be working right, and I would stumble frequently. Also my left leg felt funny, with a tingling sensation, and there were parts of it that were numb. After checking with four doctors, I discovered that the trouble was up in my neck, where a bony growth on my spine was pushing against my spinal cord. Pressure against this important bundle of nerves can cause all kinds of trouble lower down in the body. The answer was an operation, which would remove the growth. It might also weaken my spine or do other permanent damage, so that I might never fly in space again.

When I thought about the past two years since Gemini 10, I realized that my life as a "real" astronaut hadn't worked out the way I had hoped. It had been more hard work than glamour. Three of my friends had burned to death in a spacecraft, and now I was headed for major surgery. I checked into the hospital with a feeling of dread, but with a desire to see the pages of the calendar fly by so I could find out what was going to happen to me.

10

When I woke up after surgery, there was a plastic ring around my neck, my right hip hurt, and I had trouble swallowing. The ring was to hold my neck in one position, and I was to wear it twenty-four hours a day for three months. The hip pain was caused by the removal of a circular piece of bone from my hip, which had then been inserted into a hole in my spine, where it would cause new bone to grow and strengthen my spine. My throat hurt because the doctor had had to move it out of the way so he could reach my backbone. Within a week my pains had gone away, and I was released from the hospital. Now I had only to wait three months to see if my spine was growing back together properly.

In the meantime, my old crewmates Borman and Anders had been joined by Jim Lovell, who had taken my place. Their flight, instead of going out 4,000 miles, was now scheduled to fly all the way to the Moon. I was really sad that I would not be going with them, but I was even more concerned about my neck. When the three months were up, an X-ray showed that my spine was healing beautifully and was regaining full strength. It was a real relief to throw the plastic ring away. I was allowed to fly airplanes again, and I hoped to be assigned to a flight crew, but my first job was to help with the flight of Borman–Lovell–Anders to the Moon.

The only previous Apollo flight had been an Earth orbital test of the command module, and it had worked fine, but the idea of taking a command module all the way to the Moon was a bit scary. No one had ever left the gravitational pull of the Earth before, not in all history. Apollo 8, as Borman's flight was called, had to aim at a place in the sky where the Moon would be three days later. If done properly, they would barely miss the Moon as it passed a mere eighty miles in front of them, at a distance of 230,000 miles from Earth. Then it would fire its engine and slow down enough to be captured by the Moon's gravity. It would be trapped in lunar orbit unless its engine worked properly to start it on the trip back to Earth. Since none of this had been done before, people were naturally worried. My job was to work in Mission Control and to talk on the radio with the crew, relaying necessary information to them.

When launch day arrived, I was quite nervous. This was the first crew to ride the gigantic Saturn V rocket, and I wasn't sure how safe a ride it would be. I remembered watching the first flight of the unmanned Saturn V. The safety people wouldn't let spectators get within three miles of it, but even at that distance the monster made the sand shake under my feet, and the crackling roar of its five huge engines made me wince. Now three men would be not three miles away, but perched on the nose of the monster! As they left the launchpad, their actual path in the sky was calculated and compared with the ideal path, which was shown as a line on the wall in Mission Control Center. Their spacecraft appeared as a dot, which was supposed to climb up the center of the line. If the Saturn V veered off in the wrong direction, we would know it by watching the dot separate from the line. Then I would notify Borman and he could separate his command module from the Saturn V and return to Earth. Fortunately, I didn't need to do this, as the Saturn V put the spacecraft in the proper orbit. After checking all their equipment, they were ready to leave Earth orbit for the first time in history, and again the Saturn V put them on a perfect path for the Moon.

Now they were on their way, and I breathed a sigh of relief. When they got to the Moon three days later, they chattered like excited tourists. They thought the Moon looked like dirty beach sand. It was Christmas Eve, and they celebrated by reading parts of the Bible, from the Book of Genesis. It is the very first part of the Bible: "In the beginning God created the heaven and the earth, and the earth was without form and void, and darkness was upon the face of the deep; and the Spirit of God moved upon the face of the waters. And God said, 'Let there be light'; and there was light." On their way back from the Moon, Jim Lovell said he thought the Earth looked like a "grand oasis in the great vastness of space." I got the feeling from listening to them talk on the radio for a week that they would appreciate the Earth more from then on because of their flight so far away from it.

When the flight ended and the spacecraft plopped

into the Pacific Ocean, I felt both great happiness and sadness. I was happy that everything had gone so well, and sad that I had not been able to go with Borman and Anders instead of Lovell. In place of a trip to the Moon, I had only a scar on my throat and a great desire to make up for lost time.

The news was not long in coming, and it was all good. I was assigned to the Apollo 11 crew, with Neil Armstrong and Buzz Aldrin! We were to be the first crew to attempt a lunar landing, provided everything went well. By that I mean that Apollos 9 and 10 must make near-perfect flights before us. Apollo 9 was the first test flight of the lunar module, in Earth orbit, and Apollo 10 was to be a dress rehearsal in lunar orbit, involving a rendezvous but not a landing. I figured the chances were about fifty-fifty for Apollo 11 to be the first flight to try a landing. I would know in six months' time, but meanwhile it was back into the simulator for me, because that is where I would get the knowledge I needed to fly safely and well.

The simulator, inside, looked exactly like a real command module. Outside, it looked completely different. There were huge boxes attached to the windows, which contained make-believe stars and spacecraft, so that when we looked out the windows we would see what we would see in flight. Then there was a huge computer, which figured out things like how far away from the Earth or the lunar module we might be at any time in our imaginary flight. The whole thing looked like a huge pile of jumbled boxes. John Young called it the "great train wreck." Sometimes I got inside it with Neil and Buzz and we practiced things like launches and reentries, where all three of us would be together. At other times, Neil and Buzz got into a lunar-module simulator and I stayed by myself in the command-module simulator. We each had our own computer, and we would hook these up to Mission Control's computer, and then we would pretend to chase each other around the Moon while the computers measured how long it took and how much fuel we used. As the months went by, we got better and better at flying the simulator, and finally I was ready to stop pretending and really fly.

Of course, being the first lunar-landing flight made Apollo 11 different in a number of ways. One was germs. No one had ever worried about germs in empty space, but now we were going to touch the Moon. Suppose there were germs on the Moon, and suppose when we brought them back on our clothes and bodies, we discovered that they killed Earth plants or animals or people?

Very few scientists thought this could happen, but no one wanted to take a chance on infecting Planet Earth with Moon germs. Therefore, the three of us would be separated from the rest of the world until we had been certified "germ-free," or at least "Moon-germ-free" (there is no way of getting rid of the normal germs in your body). The way it would work was this: when we landed in the Pacific, we would open our side hatch, and the Navy frogmen would throw in three rubber suits to us. We would put these on before leaving the spacecraft. Since they covered head and body entirely, our germs would stay inside them. Then we would be delivered by helicopter to the aircraft carrier, where we would be locked up inside an aluminum box that looked like a house trailer. When the aircraft carrier reached Hawaii, the box (with us still inside it) would be flown to Houston and put inside a special sealed building. Then we could get out of the box, and scientists and doctors could check us for a couple of weeks. If we didn't show signs of sickness, and no strange germs could be found, then we would be released from the building.

Somehow, the possibility of germs did not worry me. Maybe that was because I had plenty of other things to think about. Newspaper reporters frequently asked us what the most dangerous part of our trip to the Moon would be, and I usually answered, "That part that we have overlooked in our preparations." In other words, if we knew something was really dangerous, we would spend more time practicing that, but in the meantime we might overlook some little detail that no one had thought about, and that could be most dangerous of all. When I thought about our eight-day voyage, it seemed to me that there were eleven major events along the way:

1. LAUNCH. Obviously a hazardous time, with gigantic engines spewing out high-temperature exhaust gases, and terrific wind blasts as the rocket ascended.

2. TLI. Translunar injection meant firing the Saturn V's engine for the final time, putting us on a course that would barely miss the Moon three days later.

3. T&D. Transposition and docking was the process by which I would fly the command module out in front of the Saturn V, turn around and dock with the lunar module nestled in the Saturn's nose, and pull the lunar module free.

4. LOI. Lunar-orbit insertion was the process of slowing down enough to be captured by the Moon's gravity, but not slow enough to crash into the Moon.

5. LUNAR-MODULE DESCENT. This was a tricky time for Neil and Buzz, to make sure they came down at exactly the right spot on the Moon.

6. LANDING. Could be very dangerous; we simply didn't know. Fuel tanks would be near empty. Dust might make it hard to see. The surface might be too rough.

7. EVA. Extra-vehicular activity—walking on the moon—might be very tiring. Neil or Buzz might fall down and injure himself or his equipment. There might even be potholes or underground weaknesses that would cause the surface to collapse under their weight.

8. LIFTOFF. Neil and Buzz's single ascent engine had better work, or they were stranded forever.

9. RENDEZVOUS. The most complicated part of all. There were eighteen different types of rendezvous that could result if various things went wrong. A lot of them involved my rescuing Neil and Buzz.

10. TEI. Trans-earth injection meant igniting the command module's engine to cause us to speed up enough to break the Moon's tug of gravity and send us on our way back to Earth.

11. ENTRY. We had to dive into the Earth's atmosphere at precisely the right angle. If the angle was too

shallow, we might skip back out of the atmosphere and miss the Earth entirely. If too steep, we could burn up.

These eleven were the major events, and they were hooked together like a fragile daisy chain looped around the Moon. If one broke, the whole chain was useless. Of course, our friends on the earlier flights had tried out as many of them as possible. Wally Schirra's crew on Apollo 7 had checked out the command module. Frank Borman on Apollo 8 had taken the command module all the way to the Moon. Jim McDivitt and his Apollo 9 crew had test flown the lunar module. Finally, Tom Stafford and Apollo 10 had conducted a rehearsal in lunar orbit, including everything but a landing.

The thing that made our flight different, in addition to the landing itself, was that this was what the whole world had been waiting for, ever since President Kennedy had set a goal, eight years before, of "landing a man on the moon and returning him safely to the earth." Flying in space was spooky enough, and I had been nervous before Gemini 10. But this time it was a different feeling. Gemini 10 had felt like a small local event compared to Apollo 11. This time I felt a great pressure on me, a pressure to not make any mistakes, because the whole world was watching. If the crew made mistakes, we would make not only ourselves look ridiculous, but also our whole country. I felt this pressure very keenly as our launch day of July 16, 1969, approached.

And, of course, I continued to make mistakes, as all humans do. I remember one night flying from Dover, Delaware, to Houston, Texas. As I passed over the familiar terrain, I glanced down at the twin cities of Baltimore and Washington, where I had gone to high school and where my mother still lived. I tried to find my old school and just about had it located when I suddenly realized I wasn't looking at Washington at all, but at Baltimore. Somehow I had turned the two cities around in my mind. And this guy who couldn't tell Washington from Baltimore when directly overhead was about to navigate to the Moon and back. No harm done, of course, but still . . . it made you wonder.

We also had a hundred little things to take care of before we flew, such as designing a mission emblem and naming our spacecraft. NASA wasn't too fond of names for spacecraft, and during the Gemini program we had used numbers only (like Gemini 10), but now we had two spacecraft, and we couldn't call them both Apollo 11 on the radio, so we needed names. Apollo 9 had called theirs *Gumdrop* and *Spider,* which I thought were neat names because the command module *was* shaped like a gumdrop and the lunar module *did* look sort of like a spider. But for Apollo 11 we wanted something that sounded a little more important. We also wanted an emblem that didn't show the spacecraft themselves but that somehow said our country was making a peaceful landing on the Moon. Our country's symbol is the eagle, and one night I traced a landing eagle out of a *National Geographic,* and sketched the Moon underneath the bird, with the Earth in the background. I made a mistake about the direction from which sunshine would be striking the Earth. The Earth should have looked like ⬤ but I drew it like ⬤ ,

and nobody discovered the mistake until after the flight. We all liked the eagle, but it didn't look too peaceful until someone suggested we put an olive branch, the symbol of peace, in its claws. Now we had our emblem. From here it was an easy step to name our lunar module *Eagle,* but the command module was a more difficult choice. Finally we settled on *Columbia,* after Christopher Columbus, who discovered America.

When July arrived, Neil, Buzz, and I moved from Houston to Cape Kennedy, where we stayed in special rooms prepared for us. The idea was that we would stay away from most people and not catch their germs, so we wouldn't get sick at the last minute. Of course, we still had to be near a lot of people every day as we worked. We also had our own cook, who tried to get us as fat as possible before launch day. One time President Nixon wanted to come have dinner with us, but a NASA doctor said he shouldn't because we might catch his germs, and he didn't come. I thought that was pretty silly.

The last couple of days before launch I also had some fun, flying a T-38. The purpose was not to have fun but to do some aerobatics and cause the fluid in my inner ears to slosh around. This sloshing was to imitate space, where weightlessness would cause the fluid in our inner ears to float. It wasn't a very good imitation, but it was better than nothing, and we wanted to do whatever we could to accustom our bodies to space. Occasionally an astronaut had become sick to his stomach in space, and we thought that doing aerobatics might help prevent this. Anyway, I did a lot of loops and rolls, and I felt fine. I was ready to go to the Moon.

11

Deke Slayton woke me up at four o'clock on the morning of July 16, 1969. Gemini 10 had been launched in the afternoon, but Apollo 11 was scheduled for an 8:32 A.M. departure, and we had a lot of things to do before then. I started with a quick shave and a shower, followed by a very brief physical exam. Then I joined Neil and Buzz and a couple of friends for the astronaut's traditional launch-day breakfast of steak and eggs. It was a bigger breakfast than I normally eat, but steak is good anytime. After breakfast, I returned to my bedroom and brushed my teeth really well. I also finished packing up my clothes. Some of them were to be delivered to my home in Houston and others were going into the germproof laboratory in which we would live for two weeks if we really did bring back some Moon rocks.

The next step was to get dressed in our pressure suits and make sure the suits weren't leaking. This procedure took nearly an hour, and then we were ready to make the eight-mile trip to the launchpad. As we left our building, several hundred people who had worked on our spacecraft were there to say goodbye, waving and shouting. Inside our sealed bubble helmets, we couldn't hear what they were saying, but we did smile and wave back. Then we climbed aboard a small van and headed for the launchpad. Tourist traffic was bumber-to-bumper and barely moving, but our van was in a special lane and we sailed on past the tourists and turned off the highway onto a small access road. We could tell from the blue sky that it was a pretty day, and we knew (because it was July in Florida) that it was hot, but inside our suits all we could feel was the cool flow of oxygen. As we approached the Saturn V, I got my usual feeling of awe as I looked up at it. It was a monster! Over three times as tall as a Gemini-Titan, taller than a football field set on end, as tall as the largest redwood tree, it was really impressive, and the closer we got, the bigger it seemed.

As our van pulled up next to the launchpad elevator, I noticed a strange thing. Every time I had been here before, the place had been a beehive of activity, with swarms of workmen everywhere, getting things ready. Now their work was done, and the place was deserted, with not a soul in sight. It was like visiting an abandoned city. Also, the rocket looked different today. Filled with kerosene fuel now, plus the super-cool liquid oxygen and hydrogen, it was steaming in the sunshine. Its sides were coated with ice, where the moist Florida air came in contact with the freezing-cold skin of the rocket in the vicinity of the liquid oxygen and hydrogen tanks. This steaming ice somehow made the rocket seem alive.

As our elevator finished its brief journey, I realized that our trip to the Moon had already begun. We had left the surface of the Earth, which of course was itself hurtling through space in its orbit around the sun. As I got off the elevator, 320 feet above the Florida sand, I could look out and see the beautiful beach and the calm blue Atlantic. If I closed my right eye, that was all I saw. But if I reversed the process, and closed my left eye, all I could see was machinery—a huge pile of it, rocket and gantry and cables and pipes all jumbled together in confusion. It was quite a contrast. I hoped someday to get back to the beach and a simpler life, but for the next eight days, part of this machinery would be my home, and I had to concentrate on it.

As Neil, Buzz, and I walked across a narrow bridge between the elevator and *Columbia*, our command module, we were greeted by a small team of men who would help us get aboard *Columbia* and then lock the hatch behind us. The team leader was Guenter Wendt, and it was an astronaut tradition to play a joke on him on launch day. For the past month, Guenter had been telling me what a great fisherman he was, and how large the trout were that he was accustomed to catching. I had located a tiny trout, the smallest one to be found, and had had the smelly thing nailed to a wooden board with a sign saying "Guenter's Trophy Trout." I took it out of a paper bag I had been carrying and presented it to Guenter as I climbed on board, and we both had a good laugh. Years later, Guenter told me he still had the trophy in his deep freezer, which I guess is the only place to keep an uncured fish.

Once inside *Columbia*, the three of us had some last-minute checks to make while Guenter and crew were departing, and then it was time for us to go. I was lying in the right-hand couch, with Buzz in the center and Neil over on the left side. If the Saturn blew up, Neil could twist a handle he held in his left hand and our spacecraft would be lifted (by three small rockets on our nose) up and away to safety. At least that was the way it was supposed to work. If during the next eight days, everything worked as advertised, then our job would be fairly simple. But I doubted that every last piece of machinery would work perfectly. There were simply too many things that could go wrong. I guessed that our chances of actually carrying off the entire flight as planned were about even. But there was no time left for worrying about such things, for now the voice on the radio was counting down to liftoff. At nine seconds before liftoff, the five first-stage engines of the Saturn ignited, and the people on the ground checked their power as it was increased to the liftoff thrust of seven and a half million pounds. When everything looked okay, the clamps holding us to the launchpad were released, and we were on our way.

There was no doubt in my mind, either, for right away the rocket engines began jerking back and forth, swiveling to keep us in balance as we climbed. We felt this as little sideways jerks, like sometimes, when you first start out on a bicycle, you have to yank the wheel back and forth to prevent tipping over. Once you pick up some speed, on a bicycle or in a rocket, you can steer more smoothly. But the first few seconds of the Saturn V were wobbly and very noisy, and I was glad when they were over.

As we climbed out over the Atlantic, I noted with satisfaction that all my dials and instruments were normal, and I could see out of the corner of my eye that Neil and Buzz were also pleased with what they saw. Buzz was checking with our computer, which indicated we were on the right flight path. After two and a half minutes, the first stage shut down and fell off into the sea, and the second stage, with its own five engines, took over. At nine minutes they, too, had finished their job and were discarded, and we were left with the single engine of the third stage to see us safely into orbit. Finally, at eleven minutes and forty-two seconds after liftoff, we arrived in orbit, one hundred miles up at a speed of 18,000 miles an hour. The first big hurdle was behind us. Only ten more to go!

In the three short years since Gemini 10, I had forgotten how beautiful the view was, as clouds and sea glided silently by my window in the pure sunlight. We were upside down, in that our heads were pointed toward the Earth and our feet toward the black sky, but since we were weightless, it didn't really matter which way we were pointed. We had picked this direction because it allowed our navigational instruments, which were in the belly of *Columbia*, to point at the stars.

Before we left the relative safety of Earth orbit, we wanted to make sure that our navigational equipment was working properly, and that meant using our sextant to sight on two stars. When it came time for me to make these star sightings, I remembered a bet I had made with one of the simulator instructors. If I took a perfect sighting, the computer would tell me that my error was 00000. We called this reading "five balls." If my reading was less accurate, the computer would start adding numbers in place of the zeros. I had bet a cup of coffee that my first reading would be perfect (00000), and the instructor had bet that I would be off by two one-hundredths of a degree (00002). When I took my sighting, I got my answer: 00001, four balls one. It was a tie, and I called Houston and said, "Tell Glenn Parker down at the Cape that he lucked out. He doesn't owe me a cup of coffee." I'm sure the people in Houston didn't have the vaguest idea what I was talking about, but they didn't admit that, and said simply that they would pass the information on.

We were over Australia now, exactly one hour after

liftoff, and all our machinery seemed to be working perfectly. We would have one more Earth orbit to make sure, and then we would be on our way to the Moon. We spent the time checking as much equipment as we could, just as we had agreed to do months before in meetings with the various experts. When the time came, on our second pass over Australia, Houston said, "You are *go* for TLI," which meant that we had permission to ignite the Saturn's third-stage engine for the second and last time. It would increase our speed from 18,000 to 25,000 miles per hour, and we would have broken the bonds of Earth's gravity. When the moment came and the engine ignited, I felt both relief and tension. Relief because without it we would never reach the Moon, and tension because now we were committed, and turning back would be almost impossible.

The third-stage engine of the Saturn had a character all its own. The first stage had been very busy, steering from side to side, while the second stage had been as smooth as glass. The third stage vibrated quite a bit, not from side to side but with a choppy fore-and-aft motion that was felt as almost a buzz. The engine's thrust pushed us back into our couches gently, with a force of slightly less than 1 G. It was a marvelous machine, which took liquid hydrogen stored at −423° and liquid oxygen at −293° and burned them seconds later at over 4000°. For almost six minutes we enjoyed this ride, and then the engine shut down automatically, and our computer told us we were headed toward that empty point in the sky where the Moon would be three days from then. "Hey, Houston," said Neil, "that Saturn gave us a magnificent ride." It was hard to believe that we had passed our second hurdle already. I bet that many of the one million people who were at Cape Kennedy to watch our launch were still caught in the post-launch traffic jam.

Inside *Columbia*, it was now time to switch our seats. I moved from right to left, with Neil now in the center and Buzz on the right. It was time for transposition and docking, the maneuver by which we would attach *Columbia* to *Eagle*, nose to nose. To do it, I had to fly *Columbia* away from the Saturn, and then turn around and come back and dock with *Eagle*. It was my first chance to fly *Columbia*, and it felt good. After separating and turning around, I approached *Eagle*, which looked like a mechanical spider crouched in its hole atop the Saturn. I brought the two vehicles together gently, with a slight bump as *Columbia*'s docking probe mated with *Eagle*'s drogue. Then I slipped down out of the couch and into *Columbia*'s tunnel, removing the docking probe as I went. I connected a couple of wires, and now *Eagle* was receiving electricity from *Columbia*. The next step was to throw a switch that separated *Eagle* from the Saturn and allowed *Eagle* and *Columbia* to float free. The poor old Saturn was finished now; it was an empty carcass destined to orbit the Sun.

With the third hurdle behind us, we still had a couple more tasks to perform before our day was over. One was very pleasant: crawling out of our pressure suits and stowing them away in bags. It made the inside of *Columbia* seem much larger. We felt safe enough in *Columbia* as long as we weren't going to pop loose from *Eagle* (which would have let all our air out), and I had checked the tunnel connections to *Eagle* several times. Once out of my suit, I did some practice navigating, finding several stars and measuring the angle between them and the Earth's horizon. Then it was time to start worrying about temperatures inside *Columbia* and *Eagle*. We were between the Earth and the Moon, in constant sunlight. If we held the spacecraft in any one position, the side facing the Sun would become too hot and the side in the shadows would become too cold. Too hot meant propellant-tank pressures rising dangerously high; too cold meant radiators freezing. To prevent either, we had to position the space-craft broadside to the Sun, and then begin to turn slowly.

Once we had this motion established, we could relax and watch the Earth and the Moon slowly parade past our windows. The Moon didn't seem to be getting much bigger, but the Earth was definitely shrinking. By the end of our first day in space, the Earth barely filled one small window. It was really bright, with the blue of the ocean and the white of the clouds being what you noticed most. The green of the jungle areas was not distinct at all, and though the rust-colored sandy deserts were quite visible, the main impression was one of clouds and sea.

We usually think of the Moon as being quite bright, especially when it is full, but the Moon is a dullard com-pared to the Earth. In technical terms, the albedo of the Moon is .07, which means that it bounces back only 7 percent of the light striking it, absorbing the other 93 percent. The Earth's albedo is four times that of the Moon, which means it shines four times as brightly. The sunshine really bounces off it, especially off the surface of the ocean, and if your eyes and the Sun are in just the right position, the ocean will sparkle and flash like a fine diamond held up to a bright light. As I got ready for bed, I tried to decide what you called where we were.

It is usually described as "cislunar space," but that really wasn't a good name for this strange region. We were in constant sunlight, which meant it was "daytime," but if you looked away from the Sun, the sky was black as pitch. No stars were visible, even though they were there, just as they always had been. The reason they could not be seen was that sunlight was flooding the inside of *Columbia*, which meant that the pupils of our eyes automatically narrowed until only very bright objects could be seen. The only way to see the stars was to block out the sunshine and allow the pupils to expand for several minutes. Then the stars would gradually reappear, but were gone in a flash if the eye was exposed to sunshine, either directly or bouncing off some part of the spacecraft.

Our second day in space was a very quiet one—the first such day I had ever known. It was pleasant to see the Earth getting smaller and smaller in our windows. There was absolutely no sensation of speed. We seemed to be just hanging there, as we went about our chores. Neil and Buzz spent most of their time studying *Eagle* checklists and procedures, while I attended to all the machinery inside *Columbia*. We ignited *Columbia*'s rocket engine once, for just three seconds, to adjust our course slightly.

The Moon was pulling us, the Earth was pulling us, and the Sun was pulling us. The result of this tug-of-war was a curved path through the sky, and a constantly changing speed. We had been slowing down ever since we left the Earth and would continue to do so until we got much closer to the Moon, at which time its gravitational field would take over and we would start speeding up again. The three-second correction put us back on the center line of our imaginary highway.

With plenty of time to prowl around inside *Columbia*, I found that weightlessness made it seem like a completely different place than it had been on the ground. On Earth, the tunnel, for example, was simply waste space overhead, but here it turned into a pleasant little nook where you could sit, or crouch, or whatever you wanted to call just being there, out of everyone else's way. I found that corners and tunnels were good places; you could wedge yourself in and did not need a lap belt or anything to hold you in place. In weightlessness, you have to be wedged in, or tied down, or your body will float aimlessly, banging into other people or equipment as it goes. At first, just floating around is great fun, but then after a while it becomes annoying, and you want to stay in one place.

Day number 2 was so quiet I even had time to do some exercise. I found a spot near the navigator's panel that was just wide enough to allow my body to stretch out, with my arms over my head touching one wall and my feet another. In this position, I could "run" in place. With my medical sensors still attached to my chest, I could find out from the people in Houston what my heart rate was. I exercised until it doubled, from fifty to one hundred beats per minute, and then I stopped, because I didn't want to get too hot or sweaty, with no bath or shower on board.

We also had a TV show on day number 2, using our TV camera to show the people back home what their puny little planet looked like from 130,000 miles away. By pointing the camera out the window at the Earth, and then turning it over in my hands, I could make the Earth appear to tumble, not something you get to do every day. I told Houston, "Okay, world, hang on to your hat. I'm going to turn you upside down."

By the time we got the TV equipment packed up and put away, it was bedtime. All three of us were relaxed by now and ready for a long snooze. It was my turn to sleep under the left couch, zipped loosely inside a floating hammock, and I was comfortable indeed, much more so than the previous night or during any of my three Gemini nights. It was a strange sensation to float in the total darkness, suspended by a cobweb's light touch, with no pressure anywhere on my body. Instinctively, I felt that I was lying on my back, not my stomach, but I really was doing neither—most normal yardsticks disappear in space, and I was no more lying than standing or falling. The only thing I could say, really, was that I was stretched out, with my body in a straight line from head to toe. The reason I thought of myself as lying on my back was that the main instrument panel was in front of me, and I had long accustomed myself to think of that direction as "up." The next thing I knew, Buzz was talking on the radio, and I realized that it was "morning"—or, at least, eight hours had passed. In the constant sunshine between Earth and Moon, it was difficult to decide whether it was "morning" or "noon" or "evening." All I knew was that the Sun was still in the sky, just as it had been when I saw it last, and the Earth was smaller yet, appearing to be about the size of my wristwatch.

Day number 3 was even quieter than day number 2, but day number 4 had an entirely different feeling to it. We knew we were going to be plenty busy and were going to see some strange sights. We stopped our barbecue motion and got our first look at the Moon in nearly a day. The change in its appearance was spectacular! The Moon I had known all my life, that small flat yellow disk in the sky, had gone somewhere, to be replaced by the most awesome sphere I had ever seen. It was huge, completely filling *Columbia*'s largest window. It was also three-dimensional, by which I mean that we could see its belly bulging out toward us, while its surface obviously receded toward the edges. I felt that I could almost reach out and touch it. It was between us and the Sun, putting us in its shadow. The Sun created a halo around it, making the Moon's surface dark and mysterious in comparison with its shining rim. Its surface was lighted by Earthshine, which was sunshine that had bounced off the surface of the Earth onto the surface of the Moon. It cast a bluish eerie glow by which we could see large craters and the darker flat areas known as maria, or seas. It didn't look like a very friendly place, but Neil summed it up: "It's worth the price of the trip." To me, it also looked a little bit scary.

In order to get into orbit around the Moon, we had to slow down, or else we would have shot right on by it. We fired *Columbia*'s rocket engine shortly after we swung around behind the Moon's left edge, out of touch with the Earth for the first time in three days. However, we didn't need the Earth, because our own computer told us which way to point and how long to fire the engine. After slightly more than six minutes of engine firing, our computer told us we had arrived, and we had! We were skimming along approximately sixty miles above the Moon's pockmarked surface.

The back side of the Moon, which we never see from Earth, is even more battered and tortured-looking than the front side. On the back, there are no smooth maria, but only highlands that have been scarred by the impact of meteorites over billions of years.

There is no atmosphere surrounding the Moon to produce clouds or smog, so our view was impaired only by darkness. We discovered that the appearance of the surface changed greatly as the position of the Sun changed. With the Sun directly overhead, the Moon appeared a cheery place, with soft rounded craters bathed in a rose-colored light. As the Sun shifted toward the lunar horizon, the craters began to cast long shadows, the rose color changed to dark gray, and the surface appeared not smooth at all, but a series of jagged edges. When the Sun was below the horizon, the surface was either barely visible if it was in Earthshine, or totally invisible in a black void if out of it.

We were really eager to get a look at our landing site. We didn't have any trouble finding it, because we had been studying maps for months and had memorized a series of craters and other checkpoints leading up to the landing site. But, boy, when we got there, it sure looked rough to me. It didn't look smooth enough to park a baby buggy, much less our landing craft, *Eagle*. I didn't say anything to Neil or Buzz. I just hoped it was the angle of the Sun that was causing the rough appearance. We would find out tomorrow.

In the meantime, I had one more task to perform before bedtime. With my sextant I took several measurements on a crater in the Foaming Sea (Mare Spumans, in Latin) east of our landing site in the Sea of Tranquillity. The idea was that my measurements could increase the accuracy of our knowledge of the height of the terrain Neil and Buzz would be flying over in their descent to a landing. I had named the crater KAMP, using the first letters of the names of my family (Kate, Ann, Michael, and Patricia). I liked the idea of my wife and kids being involved with helping the lunar landing.

The next day, number 5, lunar-landing day, began with the usual wake-up call from Houston, and proceeded swiftly from there. It was while we were eating breakfast that Houston told us the story of the Chinese woman and rabbit that I mentioned at the beginning of this book. As soon as breakfast was over, we had to scramble into our pressure suits. Neil and Buzz began by putting on special underwear, into which thin plastic tubes had been woven. Water would be pumped from their back-packs into their suits and through these tubes, cooling their bodies while they were out on the hot lunar surface. Since I would not be joining them there, I wore plain old regular underwear, or "long johns," as they are called. When we unpacked the three pressure suits from their bags, they seemed almost to fill the entire command module, as if there were three extra people in there with us. After quite a struggle and a tug-of-war with a balky zipper, we finally got the suits on and our helmets and gloves locked in place. Then Neil and Buzz entered the lunar module, and I locked the hatch after them. I threw a switch on my instrument panel, and our two spacecraft separated.

Neil backed off fifty feet or so and made a slow 360° turn in front of me. The idea was to allow me to inspect all sides of the lunar module for possible damage, and to make sure all four landing gear were extended properly. I couldn't find anything wrong with *Eagle*, but it sure looked strange, unlike any kind of flying machine I had ever seen. It looked like a huge gold, black, and gray bug hanging awkwardly in the black sky. But Buzz was pleased with it. "The *Eagle* has wings!" he shouted. To me, it didn't look like an eagle, and I couldn't find any wings, only lumps and bumps and odd shapes on its surface. Since a lunar module flies only in space, high above the Earth's atmosphere, the designers didn't have to make it streamlined, which is the reason it looked so awkward.

As Neil and Buzz descended to the lunar surface, I kept my eyes on them as long as I could. If they had to come back in a hurry for any reason, I wanted to know where they were. Looking at them through my sextant, I watched *Eagle* grow smaller and smaller until finally, when it was about one hundred miles away (below me and in front of me), I lost sight of it amid the craters.

My main job now was to keep *Columbia* running properly, and to keep quiet, because *Eagle* and Houston would have plenty to talk about during the landing attempt. Sure enough, it wasn't long before I could hear Neil telling Houston his computer was acting strangely, and Houston promptly replied that he should continue toward a landing. Buzz was calling off numbers to Neil, so that Neil could devote all his attention to looking out the window. The most important numbers were altitude (in feet above the surface) and descent rate (in feet per second). "Six hundred feet, down at nineteen . . . Four hundred feet, down at nine . . . Three hundred feet . . . Watch our shadow out there," called Buzz, repeating new numbers every few seconds. He also reported they had only 5 percent of their fuel remaining, which wasn't much. I started getting nervous. "Forty feet, down two and a half, kicking up some dust." Well, at least the dust didn't seem to be a big problem; that was good. "Thirty seconds!" said Houston, meaning that they had only thirty seconds' worth of fuel remaining. Better get it on the ground, Neil!

Suddenly Buzz shouted: "Contact light!" and I knew they were down. The lunar module had a wire dangling below one landing gear. When it touched the Moon, it caused a light on the instrument panel to light, so that Neil would know he was just about to touch down. As soon as he did, he called, "Houston, Tranquillity Base here. The *Eagle* has landed." Whew! I breathed a big sigh of relief. Neil then explained why he had nearly run out of gas. The computer-controlled descent was taking *Eagle* into an area covered with huge boulders, and Neil had to keep flying until he found a smoother spot to land. As good as that computer was, it took the eyes of the pilot to pick the best landing spot.

For the next couple of orbits, I tried very hard to spot *Eagle* through my sextant, but I was unable to find it. The problem was that no one knew exactly where Neil had landed, and I didn't know which way to look for them. Oh, I knew approximately where they were, but the sextant had a narrow field of view, like looking down a rifle barrel, and I needed to know exactly which way to point it.

Other than not being able to find Neil and Buzz, everything was going very well with me. I had turned up the lights inside *Columbia*, and it seemed like a happy place. Also big, for a change, with only me inside it. I didn't feel lonely or left out, because I knew my job was very important, and that Neil and Buzz could never get home without me. I was proud of the way *Columbia* and I were circling above them, waiting for their return. I felt like the base-camp operator on a mountain-climbing expedition.

I suppose one reason I didn't feel lonely was that I had been flying airplanes by myself for nearly twenty years. This time, however, I had to admit that it *was* a bit different, especially on the far side of the Moon. There, cut off from all communication, I was truly alone, the only person in the solar system who could not even see the planet of his birth. Far from causing fear, this situation gave me a good feeling—one of confidence and satisfaction. Outside my window I could see stars, and nothing else. I knew where the Moon was, but in the total darkness, its surface was not visible: it was simply that part of my window that had no stars in it. The feeling was less like flying than like being alone in a boat on the ocean at night. Stars above, pure black below.

At dawn, light filled my windows so quickly that my eyes hurt. Almost immediately, the stars disappeared and the Moon reappeared. I knew from my clock that the Earth was about to reappear, and right on schedule it popped into view, rising like a blue-and-white jewel over the desolate lunar horizon.

As soon as the Earth reappeared, I could once more talk on my radio, and I found out from Houston that all was going well with Neil and Buzz. They had decided to skip a scheduled four-hour nap and instead began exploring right away. Neil, first down the ladder and therefore the first human to take an extraterrestrial step, found he had no difficulty at all in walking on the Moon. The surface was level and solid and firm, and he easily kept his balance in the strange gravitational field where everything weighed only one sixth its Earth weight. I could hear what they were saying because Houston relayed their calls to me. It was a bit unusual, though, because even traveling at the speed of light, it took two and a half seconds for the radio signals to go from *Eagle* to the Earth and then back to *Columbia.* If they said something to me, they had to wait at least five seconds for an answer. When I was overhead their position, I could talk to them directly, but the rest of the time that I was on the front side of the Moon, the relay procedure was necessary. When I was on the back side, I couldn't talk to anyone.

They hadn't been out on the surface very long when the three of us got a big surprise. The president of the United States began talking on the radio! Mr. Nixon told them, "Neil and Buzz, I am talking to you by telephone from the Oval Office at the White House, and this certainly has to be the most historic telephone call ever made . . . Because of what you have done, the heavens have become a part of man's world. As you talk to us from the Sea of Tranquillity, it inspires us to redouble our efforts to bring peace and tranquility to Earth." Neil replied that he was honored and privileged to be on the

Moon, representing the United States and men of peace from all nations. I felt proud to be representing my country, and I was glad that Neil and Buzz had planted an American flag on the Moon. Now I just wanted them to collect their rocks and get back on up to *Columbia*. They really sounded good on the surface, not tired at all, but I was still relieved when they got back inside *Eagle* and got the door locked. That was another big hurdle behind us, and none of us, we hoped, would need our pressure suits again. In the meantime, we were scheduled to sleep for a few hours, so that we would be fresh for the complicated rendezvous.

I know Neil and Buzz didn't sleep very well, cramped on the narrow floor of *Eagle*, but I had a good rest in *Columbia*. I blocked out all the light by putting shades over the windows, and I trusted the experts in Houston to watch over my equipment while I was asleep. Of course, if anything went wrong on the far side of the Moon no one could help me, but on the front side Houston could tell from *Columbia*'s electronic signals whether most things were working properly or not. If trouble developed, they could call me on the radio and wake me up. Reassured by this, I slept like a log, until I heard a voice in my ear, calling over and over again: "*Columbia, Columbia*, good morning from Houston." "Hi, Ron," I replied groggily. It was Ron Evans, an astronaut who would later fly to the Moon on the final Apollo flight. Ron told me it was going to be a busy day, which I knew already, and then he proved it by giving me a long list of things to do to prepare for the rendezvous. As the day wore on, I knew I would be expected to perform approximately 850 computer-button pushes alone. If everything went well with *Eagle*, I knew precisely what to do, because I had practiced over and over again in the simulator, but if I had to go rescue *Eagle* from some lopsided orbit, then things could get awfully complicated in a big hurry. I had a book around my neck, fastened by a clip to my pressure suit, that contained procedures for eighteen different types of rendezvous that I might need.

As *Eagle*'s liftoff time approached, I got really nervous, probably as nervous as I got at any time during the flight. If their engine didn't work, there was nothing I could do to rescue them from the surface. I simply had to come home by myself, leaving Neil and Buzz to die on the surface of the Moon. They had oxygen enough for only another day at the most. Needless to say, the idea of leaving them was horrible, but it was the only thing I could do, as it made no sense for me to commit suicide. These

This portrait was taken on January 10, 1969, the day after the announcement of the Apollo 11 crew assignment. From left to right are lunar module pilot Buzz Aldrin, commander Neil Armstrong, and a beaming command module pilot.

Worrying about the Apollo 11 mission before it even launched.

Apollo 11 liftoff as
viewed from the
launch tower.

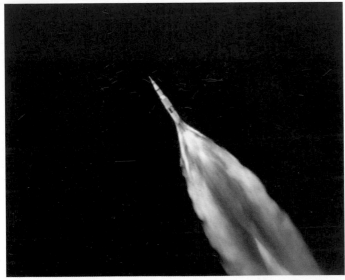

Our ascent
photographed
from an Air Force
EC-135.

Our first glimpse of the *Eagle*, nestled in the top of the empty Saturn V.

The *Eagle* gets a chance to test its wings.

A most famous picture taken by Neil of Buzz.
(See Neil's reflection in the visor?)

A strange but beautiful setting for the American flag.

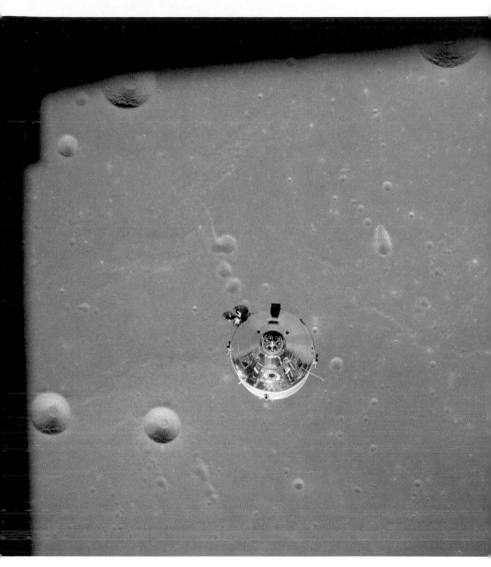

A head-on view of *Columbia*, my happy home for eight days.

The most welcome sight of my life: Neil and Buzz returning to *Columbia* from the surface of the Moon.

After leaving the capsule, we put on protective gear with a Navy diver looking on.

Journey's end. The three of us inside the mobile quarantine facility, talking with the president, with whom we've just exchanged a joke.

thoughts were running through my mind as I heard Buzz counting the seconds to ignition: *"nine, eight, seven, six, five* . . . Beautiful!" They were off! Seven minutes later, their single engine had pushed them into a good orbit, below and behind me, and they then began a carefully calculated three-hour chase to close the gap. On my first pass over Tranquillity Base since their departure, I told them, *"Eagle, Columbia* passing over the landing site. It sure is great to look down there and not see you!" Not that I had ever really seen them on the surface, but just knowing they were up in orbit again was a great relief. Not long after this, I really did see *Eagle* for the first time in a day, as it appeared as a tiny blinking light in my sextant. As it grew, so did my confidence, for my computer told me they were precisely on centerline as they overtook me. Finally we were side by side, and *Eagle* had never looked better. It was missing its bottom half, which stayed on the Moon, after acting as a launching pad for the top half.

For the first time in six months, I felt that the Apollo 11 flight was definitely going to be a success. All I had to do now was dock with *Eagle,* transfer Neil and Buzz back into *Columbia,* and head for home! The docking itself went well, with just a slight bump as *Columbia* nudged

Eagle, but then *Eagle* gave a wild lurch and for a couple of seconds I thought we might have real trouble. But the two vehicles swung back in line, and then the docking latches pulled them together in a tight grip, and all was well again. Buzz was first through the hatch, with a triumphant grin on his face. I was going to kiss him, but I just shook his hand. Together we greeted Neil, and for a couple of minutes the three of us just floated there, admiring two shiny silver boxes filled with Moon rocks. I also got a couple of questions answered, such as what did the liftoff from the Moon feel like ("There was a little blast . . . The floor came up to meet you"), and did the Moon rocks all look the same ("No, not at all").

Then it was time to leave *Eagle* in lunar orbit, light *Columbia*'s big engine for a couple of minutes, and come on home. Just as in the case of a Gemini deorbit burn, we paid extraordinary attention to the direction we were pointed. If we made a mistake and pointed in the opposite direction, we would crash into the Moon instead of returning to Earth. After the burn was over, Houston told us their radar tracking stations indicated we were right on course. Another hurdle behind us! We tried to use up all our remaining film by taking pictures of the

Moon. All together, we must have taken close to a thousand pictures of it in the three days we were there. As we left the Moon, we curved around its right side, and we could see it gleaming in the sunlight, vividly etched against the black sky in gray-tan tones. It was beautiful, but it was nothing compared to Earth, and I didn't want to come back to the Moon.

The trip home was quiet and uneventful. I spent my time doing routine housekeeping chores, like adding chlorine to the drinking water, and watching the Moon get smaller and the beautiful Earth grow larger and more inviting as each hour went by. Things were so quiet that we even got to play some music we had brought along on a small tape recorder. My favorite song on the tape was called "Everyone's Gone to the Moon." Also on the tape was a recording of a bunch of loud noises: bells, train whistles, shrieks, and other unidentified sounds. At one point we played this part to the people in Houston just to shake them up. Who ever heard of train whistles coming from outer space? They were really surprised, and we wouldn't admit that we had made the noises.

We also appeared on a couple of television shows, hoping to give people an idea of what the Earth looked like, and what it was like living inside the command module in weightlessness. For instance, on one show I filled a spoon carefully with water. I told Houston, "I'm afraid I filled it too full and it's going to spill over the sides. I'll tell you what. I'll just turn this one over and get rid of the water and start all over again. Okay?" "Okay," said Houston. Slowly I turned the spoon upside down, but of course in weightlessness the water didn't spill, it stayed right in the spoon, which I then put in my mouth. I also showed the people on Earth how our water gun worked, holding it out in front of me a foot or so and squirting the water into my mouth. Or at least squirting some of it into my mouth. Most of it missed and floated off in small spherical blobs.

We had just one more hurdle to clear: that of landing safely in the ocean. We were scheduled to come down in an empty part of the South Pacific, where the aircraft carrier *Hornet* was waiting for us. President Nixon was also on the *Hornet*. As we approached the Earth, our speed really started to build up, so that we were going 25,000 miles per hour by the time we plunged back into the atmosphere at a very shallow angle of 6°. Again we ran through our checklist with great precision, because we knew we had only one chance to make a good entry. I was flying *Columbia* from the left side, with Neil in the center handling the computer, and Buzz reading the checklist from the right. We were pointed backward with our heat shield forward. We were looking out the windows at the black sky above us.

As we began to penetrate the thin upper atmosphere, the sky out our windows started to change from the black of space to a tunnel of light. We were trailing a comet's tail of light, orange-yellow in the center, with edges of blue-green and lavender. It was a spectacular sight, which grew in intensity as the air became denser. Finally the tunnel expanded and its core became so brilliant that I felt we were in the center of a gigantic million-watt light bulb. We could be seen for many hundreds of miles as we arced across the predawn Pacific sky.

As black changed to bright, so also did weightlessness give way to deceleration. It began gently, nudging us back into our couches, and then built uncomfortably. After eight days at zero G, our bodies weren't accustomed to gravity or deceleration, and our good old Earth 1 G seemed heavy indeed. By the time the force peaked at 6.5 G, I felt that a gigantic hand was pushing against my chest. But it didn't last long, and I had other things to occupy my attention. It was time for our two small drogue parachutes to open, to slow us down enough, and to hold us steady enough, to release our three main parachutes. When the drogues came out, they jerked back and forth quite a bit, but then the three huge main parachutes (each eighty feet in diameter) replaced them, and we were floating serenely down toward what we hoped was a calm sea.

I had bet Neil that when *Columbia* hit the water it would not turn over. Some Apollo command modules turned over, and others didn't. It depended on a lot of things, but the most important item was to jettison the parachutes swiftly, before the wind could catch in them and pull the spacecraft sideways, causing it to topple upside down. On the other hand, we had to be a hundred percent certain not to jettison the parachutes *before* the spacecraft hit the water. The procedure was for Buzz (the instant after we hit the water) to turn on the electricity going to the parachute release, and then I would throw the switches to release the chutes. I was thinking about this when all of a sudden—*SPLAT!*—we hit the water like a ton of bricks. Buzz's arm was jerked downward, and before he could move it back up to his electrical panel, I felt us begin to topple over. *Drat!* Neil had won again.

Anyway, it felt good to be back on Earth, even if

we were upside down. Being upside down was no big problem, either. All it meant was that I had to throw a couple of switches, which would fill rubber bags on our noses with air, and then we would slowly topple back upright. For the few minutes this took, it felt strange to be hanging against our straps with the windows filled with green water. Once we were upright again, some swimmers who had been dropped into the ocean by one of the *Hornet*'s helicopters surrounded us and tied a life raft to our side. Then we opened the hatch, and one of them threw the three biological isolation garments in to us, which we put on. These were supposed to keep any Moon germs inside with us, so that we would not contaminate the world. They were also very hot. We got out of *Columbia*, and locked the hatch behind us. Then, in the raft, we washed one another down with disinfectant, just in case any germs might be on the outside of our garments. Then, one by one, we climbed into a little wire basket on the end of a cable and were hoisted up into the helicopter.

I stood inside the helicopter and walked around a little bit. It felt kind of strange to be back in the clutch of gravity again. My body felt heavy, especially my legs. I also felt slightly tired and lightheaded. I knew from talking to other astronauts and from my own Gemini flight that this feeling was normal and would pass within an hour or so. The problem was that my heart, veins, and arteries had gotten used to weightlessness and needed a little while to readjust to gravity. Blood was pooling in my lower body because my cardiovascular system had forgotten what it was like to pump blood "uphill," there being neither "up" nor "down" in space. That was why I felt tired and lightheaded. By this time the helicopter had reached the *Hornet* and it was time to get off. I was really glad of that, because I was getting so hot inside my garment that I was about to rip it open, germs or no germs.

The helicopter landed on a big elevator which was lowered below decks. As we stepped out of it, I could barely see through my sweaty, fogged visor. I could see that there were a lot of sailors standing around, and a brass band playing. I could also barely make out the open door of the mobile quarantine facility, our next home, and I headed for it. Once sealed inside, the three of us were able to get out of our hot suits and take showers for the first time in eight days. It really felt good to be clean for a change. The mobile quarantine facility was a modified house trailer with all the doors and windows sealed, to keep any Moon germs inside. As soon as we got on board the *Hornet*, it started steaming as fast as it could for Hawaii, where the MQF would be transferred to a cargo jet for the trip back to Houston. In the meantime, we didn't have much to do except relax. President Nixon made a speech outside our window, and so did the captain of the *Hornet*, and then we ate a huge steak and got a good night's sleep. I felt heavy lying in bed instead of floating free as I had been doing for the past week. It's too bad you can't turn gravity off and on at your pleasure. That would really be fun.

In Hawaii, at Pearl Harbor, our MQF was hoisted by a huge crane onto a flat-bed truck and driven out to the airport. People were lined up along the road, shouting and waving at us, and one young man, perhaps twelve years old, ran along behind us for several miles. I wondered how he was going to get back home, and whether he would be in trouble with his parents. I hoped not, because he sure was a good runner, with a lot of endurance and determination. The trip back to Houston was kind of boring, but it was nice to get there and see our friends and families. Of course, they couldn't come inside the MQF, and we couldn't go out, so mostly we just waved at each other through the glass. Then another truck ride, from the airport a few miles over to the NASA center, where the MQF was placed inside a huge building called the lunar receiving laboratory.

The lunar receiving laboratory was designed to subject us and our Moon rocks to every possible test to make sure we had not brought any germs back from the Moon. We had to stay in it (along with a dozen people who worked there) for two weeks if no germs were discovered. If Moon germs were found? Who knows, we might have been there for the rest of our lives. In addition to physical examinations for us and microscopic checks of the rocks, there was a colony of white mice that was used to check for germs. These mice had been born in the laboratory and for all their lives they had been kept free of external germs. The idea was to expose the mice to the Moon rocks. If the mice stayed healthy, then the Moon rocks must be safe and we were free to rejoin our families without fear of infecting anyone. As the days passed and the mice stayed healthy, our spirits rose, and finally, on August 10, 1969, the flight of Apollo 11 ended and we were released to the world.

12

The success of Apollo 11 ended a remarkable part of my life. For quite a while afterward, my life really was different than it had been before. I received mail from all over the world, from ordinary people and from kings, from a few people I knew and from thousands I did not know. I got a nice letter from Charles Lindbergh, who thought that my flight around the Moon by myself must have been similar to his solo flight across the Atlantic Ocean. I heard from the children of Phil Nowlan, the man who used to write the comic strip *Buck Rogers*. They said that when they were growing up in a small Pennsylvania town, their father told them all about exploring the Moon, thirty years before it actually happened.

In addition to receiving all this mail, and honorary membership in such strange-but-wonderful-sounding organizations as the Camel Drivers Radio Club of Kabul, Afghanistan, I found that life had changed in other ways for Neil, Buzz, and me. People wanted to see and hear us. We addressed a joint session of Congress, a rare occasion in the Capitol, attended by members of the Senate, the House of Representatives, the Supreme Court, and the president's Cabinet. We followed this with a speedy trip around the world, covering twenty-five countries in thirty-eight days. Everywhere we went, people received us with great enthusiasm and said, "Well, we finally did it," meaning that we humans had finally reached the surface of another world. I was surprised by this. I had expected people in other countries to say, "Well, you Americans finally did it," but instead they said "we." It was a nice feeling.

After the world trip was over, I left the space program. It was difficult to decide to quit my job as an astronaut, but I thought I had a few good reasons. First, if I had stayed, it would have taken a couple of years to get another flight. Second, during those years, I would have continued to be away from my family a lot, and I was getting very tired of that. Third, after Apollo 11, I didn't think I would be able to keep my enthusiasm high enough to put up with the motel life, long hours, and hard work. Finally, there were plenty of other astronauts waiting to get their first flight. After I quit, my life slowly began returning to normal, and I had time to think about flying in space and what it had meant to me.

I will never forget how beautiful the Earth appears from a great distance, floating silently and serenely like a blue-and-white marble against the pure black of space. Tiny—your thumb held at arm's length can blot it out. For some reason, it also appears very fragile, as if a giant hand could suddenly reach out and crush it. Of course, there is no one giant hand, but there are billions of smaller hands on Earth working furiously to change their home. Some of the changes being made are good, and others, bad. Newspapers and books spread knowledge, but require trees to be chopped down. It seems that nearly every advance in our civilization has some undesirable side effects. Today's young people are going to have to acquire the wisdom to make sure that future changes help our planet, not hurt it, so that it becomes the beautiful, clean, blue-and-white pea it seems to be when viewed from the Moon. The Earth truly is fragile, in the sense that its surface can easily shift from blue and white to black and brown. Is the riverbank a delightful spot for watching diving ducks, or is it a lifeless, greasy stretch of muck littered with bottles and tires? As more people fly in space and get the chance to see the fragile Earth as it appears from afar, maybe that will help bring attention to some of our earthly problems.

People have always been inquisitive, have always wanted to visit new and different places, and have always gone wherever they have been able to go. Early humans were not content to remain in their native lands, but pushed onward to settle new domains. Then, once humans had no more territory to explore, they began inventing ways to leave their homeland, first on wings and later on rockets, until finally, in July 1969, they touched the face of the Moon.

Outward bound, past the Moon, these voyages will continue.

There were five more Moon landings after Apollo 11. Each one landed at a spot geologists thought looked interesting, where the rock formations might contain new information about the structure of the Moon. The last three flights carried a dune buggy, the Lunar Roving Vehicle, a lightweight battery-powered car that enabled the astronauts to travel several miles from their point of landing.

Most of the rocks brought back from the Moon were basalt, a dark, smooth stone formed by the cooling of molten lava. These rocks have helped scientists understand how the Moon was formed, but doubts still persist. The most popular theory is that, about four billion years ago, a huge object collided with the Earth, and the Moon was formed from the resulting debris.

After Apollo 17, the last manned Moon landing, some of the Apollo hardware was used in Earth orbit. The upper stage of the Saturn V Moon rocket was converted into living quarters for three astronauts. About the size of a three-bedroom house, this space station, called *Skylab*, orbited the Earth for six years on a journey that covered nearly one billion miles. Three crews lived aboard *Skylab*, the longest for eighty-four days. The nine men spent their time doing experiments that increased our knowledge of the Sun, the surface of the Earth, and the human body. The final flight of the Apollo series took place in 1975, when a command module made a rendezvous with a Soviet Soyuz spacecraft. Hooked together in Earth orbit, the group of three astronauts and two cosmonauts got along fine. Since the Soviet Union and the United States were not friendly at that time, this flight showed that people with something in common, in this case flying, can quickly become friends, even if their governments have different points of view.

For nearly six years, between 1975 and 1981, no American astronauts flew in space. Then my old friend John Young, along with Bob Crippen, made the first flight of a strange new machine, the space shuttle. It was so named because it was designed to shuttle back and forth between Cape Canaveral, in Florida, and Earth orbit. Previously, all spacecraft had been designed to fly only once and then be retired. But the shuttle, half spacecraft and half airplane, could be used over and over again. It was launched vertically, attached to rockets, but its wings allowed it to glide back to a runway and land like an airplane.

After more than fifty successful flights, disaster struck the shuttle *Challenger* in 1986 when a hole burned through the side of a solid rocket booster, causing a gigantic explosion. All seven crew members died, including Christa McAuliffe, a high school teacher from Concord, New Hampshire. Christa was to have been the first teacher in space and was going to conduct televised classes from *Challenger*. The seven deaths were the first since Virgil "Gus" Grissom, Edward White, and Roger Chaffee perished in a launchpad fire nearly twenty years previously. In both cases, the losses came as a shock to NASA and the American people. The shuttle was grounded for nearly three years while NASA made changes to improve its safety. Its career finally ended in 2003 with the crash of *Columbia*, which killed seven more.

Besides killing fourteen people, the shuttle was a disappointment in that it was more expensive to operate than its fans had hoped. On the other hand, it was also very useful, not only in putting satellites into orbit, but also in bringing them back to Earth for repair or replacement.

It seems to me that the idea behind the shuttle was a good one: a space machine that can be used repeatedly. Many studies have been made of an "aerospace plane" that could do more than the shuttle with improved reliability and lower cost.

The twenty-first century could see even larger objects in Earth orbit. Perhaps even a small town could be assembled piece by piece. It could include facilities for food production, health care, manufacturing, leisure activities—just like a town on Earth does. The main difference, of course, is that this tiny town would be circling the Earth every two hours or so. For over half this time, it would be in direct sunlight, and the energy coming from the Sun could be put to use on a regular schedule, without having to worry about whether it was a cloudy day or not: all clouds would be far below. The Sun's energy could be used to generate electricity, to heat the town, and to grow crops. Solar energy is not only abundant (and free), but also clean, unlike other popular sources, such as coal.

But one big problem for this orbital town would be where to get water. At first, water would have to be brought from Earth, and then it would have to be recycled so it could be used over and over again. The town would be sealed against the vacuum of space, and very little air or water would be allowed to escape. Both would be purified and used repeatedly. As the animals and people in the town breathed, they would use up oxygen and produce carbon dioxide. The plants grown for food would do just the opposite (using carbon dioxide and producing oxygen), keeping the entire system in balance.

Using the same water and air over and over again

sounds terribly complicated, and a little bit messy, but it's really not such an outlandish idea. After all, that is what happens here on Earth. For example, when dirty dishwater goes down the drain and into the sewer system, it enters a purification process that takes it to the ocean, where the sun's heat causes it to evaporate and enter the atmosphere, where it cools and falls back down onto the land as rain. Then the water works its way into a stream and then a reservoir and finally is pumped back into the sink to be used as dishwater once again. In space, it would be easier to recycle dirty water—and even urine—back into potable (a strange word, but look it up) water.

Will such a village ever get built in Earth orbit? Probably not. People's interest seems to be going outward, far beyond Earth. For example, there are a few interesting empty places in our solar system where the pulls of the Earth, Moon, and Sun cancel each other out. They are called libration points, and if you put a space station there—it doesn't matter how big—it will stay there. Make it a city and call it Libra. Go live there and have a good time in weightlessness.

Two very important elements in our lives on Earth are carbon and nitrogen, and we would also need them on

Libra. They are found in all living plants and animals. Carbon joins with oxygen to form carbon dioxide, which plants need to live, and nitrogen is in the air we breathe and the fertilizer we need to grow crops. Unfortunately, Libra's supply would have to come from the Earth or some other place. Perhaps a trip from Libra to one of the asteroids would bring back materials rich in carbon and nitrogen.

Life on Libra could be as interesting and varied as life on Earth. At first, Librans would consider themselves Earth people, but after a while they would probably begin to think of themselves as slightly different. In time, they truly would become different, as their bodies adapted to their new environment. In the reduced gravity of Libra, they would not need the heavy muscles of Earth people, so children growing up on Libra would tend to be slimmer (especially in the legs) than if they had been living on Earth. Their bodies would also become less tolerant of heat and cold, for Libra would not experience the extremes of temperature that we find in Alaskan winters and Arizona summers. If they visited Earth, Librans would also find windstorms most startling and unpleasant compared to the gentle air currents they knew. As a matter of fact, they would probably find the raw, uncontrolled conditions on Earth too primitive for their tastes: "A nice place to visit, but I certainly wouldn't want to live there!" they'd say. Since harmful organisms (poison ivy, jellyfish, measles, some germs, etc.) would have been prevented from entering Libra, a trip to Earth for Librans could be dangerous indeed, because their bodies would be more susceptible to Earth's infectious diseases. They might die from those diseases, or carry them back to Libra and infect others. It might be necessary for visiting Librans to wear germ-proof space suits, just as we Apollo astronauts did.

Apollo set a precedent for the future in another interesting way. It was probably the only major human expedition in which no weapons were carried. In similar fashion, no weapons would be permitted on Libra, and Librans simply would not be able to understand why Earth people continued to shoot one another.

On Libra, if people felt hostile, they would be urged to put their energies into athletic contests or other competitive events, or simply to let off steam by going flying. Libran sport flying machines would be powered by muscles. On Earth, a few people have been able to build muscle-powered airplanes that can overcome our heavy gravity for a short time, but on Libra it would be possible for a muscle-powered machine to stay aloft indefinitely. The machines would be a cross between a bicycle and a glider—a winged bicycle with a propeller. The flier's legs would provide the power to keep the propeller turning, while their hands would control elevators, ailerons, and rudders. With a little practice, Librans could learn to soar and to wheel to their heart's content, both for recreation and as a practical method of traveling across their miniature country. Life on Libra would be pleasant.

Or you might prefer to go to the Moon, or on to Mars. Those are the two choices that NASA is pursuing today. I would prefer that we bypass the place we have already visited and go directly to Mars. But my friend Neil Armstrong, who was a better engineer than I am, thought otherwise. He felt a lunar colony was a desirable (and perhaps even necessary) small step (no pun intended) before we set up house on a place as far away as Mars.

The design of a colony on either the Moon or Mars will be a fascinating project. It will have to be sealed to keep its atmosphere from escaping into the vacuum of space. But a colony could easily be built under a dome. Probably most of it would be underground, to protect people from solar radiation. The back side of the Moon—the side always away from the Earth—would be a great spot for an observatory. On the Earth, astronomers are hindered by electric lights and radio signals that pollute the night sky, but on the back side of the Moon, astronomers could view the universe without interference. Another possible location for a settlement would be down inside a crater near the Moon's South Pole, where the Sun's hot rays and dangerous solar radiation could not enter.

Venturing beyond the Moon, we can travel toward the Sun or away from it. Two planets are nearer to the Sun than Earth is, but neither Mercury nor Venus is fit for humans. Both are way too hot. Mercury has almost no atmosphere and a daytime surface temperature—800°F—that would melt lead. Venus has a very dense but unbreathable atmosphere, and a human on its surface would be crushed by the air pressure.

Two prominent Americans, Jeff Bezos and Elon Musk, are entering the debate over our next major move. Musk emphasizes Mars and wants to create a colony there, with a first flight of a hundred people. Bezos is focusing on a lunar colony where manufacturing can be done without polluting Earth. I like Musk's audacious approach to Mars, but the test pilot in me says a first crew of six or so makes better sense than going all out with one hundred. I agree with almost everything I know about Bezos, but not his overall approach to exploration. He says conditions on Earth will become so intolerable that we must escape and go do our dirty work on the Moon. He says an Earth that is static in its population and manufacturing is a very bad thing. I fall back on my fervent hope, often expressed, that we can create prosperity without growth. Stasis: bah, he says. Olé! I say. I believe the human urge to explore will propel us "outward bound," as in Tennyson's poem. I don't think we should just keep on making such a mess of things here that we have to leave. I think I will get a bumper sticker: "STASIS is my BASIS."

As we move out away from the Sun, our nearest neighbor is Mars. It, not the Moon, is where I wanted to go as a child. Thank you, Buck Rogers; I have never lost my interest in it, and in 1990 I even wrote a book about it, *Mission to Mars*. I'm delighted to see a trip to the Red Planet being discussed more lately.

Mars is in an almost circular orbit around the Sun, at a distance of about 142 million miles. The Earth's orbit is closer to the Sun, at approximately 93 million miles.

Since the Earth and Mars orbit the Sun independently of each other, there are times when the two are as close together as 49 million miles (142 – 93) or as far away as 235 million miles (142 + 93).

Because the orbits of both the Earth and Mars are slightly lopsided (elliptical rather than perfectly round), these numbers aren't exact. Once every dozen years or so, Earth and Mars actually get within 35 million miles of each other. To travel from Earth to Mars, you must aim not at Mars, but at the point in the sky where Mars will be upon your arrival. We did the same thing with the Moon on Apollo, but in that case we had to lead the Moon by only three days' positioning. In the case of Mars, the trip can take as long as nine months, following a curving arc approximately 460 million miles long. The plan might look like this:

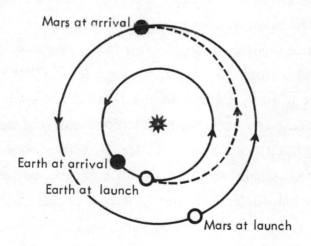

The dotted line represents the 460 million–mile journey. To travel a shorter arc requires less time, but more fuel. Upon our arrival at Mars, the Earth would be approximately 200 million miles away, which means that radio signals (traveling at the speed of light) would take nearly twenty minutes to make the trip, one way. Therefore, it would take our Mars astronauts forty minutes to ask for, and receive, any advice from Earth. That means they had better be able to solve most problems on their own, especially problems involving the Mars landing itself, where the situation might change drastically minute by minute. On the other hand, just as in the Apollo program, the big Earth-based computers would be helpful in keeping our Mars spacecraft on course, and in avoiding obstacles such as Mars's two moons, Phobos and Deimos, along the way.

Once safely on the surface of Mars, what would our astronauts find? No one can say for sure, and that is part of the reason for going. Mars has fascinated people for centuries, and they have made countless wild guesses about it. First called the Red Planet by early astronomers, Mars is actually sandy orange in color. Its diameter is about half the Earth's, and its surface is desert-like and marked by huge mountains and deep canyons. One mountain, a volcano called Olympus Mons, is 16 miles high and 374 miles across. A canyon named Valles Marineris is four miles deep—four times as deep as Arizona's Grand Canyon.

Mars has days and nights of about the same length as ours, and seasons that last twice as long. At night the temperature is bitterly cold, as much as −200°F, but at noontime, near the equator, it can reach a comfortable 65°F. Mars has an atmosphere, but a very thin one that is composed mostly of carbon dioxide, so astronauts would have to bring their own oxygen to breathe. Very high winds have been recorded on the surface of Mars, and sometimes nearly the entire surface of the planet is obscured by blowing dust. However, the atmosphere is so thin that the astronauts would not have to worry about being blown over: a fierce hurricane on Mars would push against them with about the same force as a gentle breeze on Earth. Because Mars is smaller than the Earth, Mars's gravity is not as strong—only one third that of Earth. But for a long stay, light gravity is better than none. Studies aboard the space station indicate that weightlessness can cause bone deterioration, and even some eye problems.

A typical male astronaut would weigh around sixty

pounds on Mars, and a female astronaut forty pounds. That might be a good argument for an all-female crew. It wouldn't take as much fuel to lift the lighter person from the surface, and besides, during the voyage a small woman probably wouldn't eat as much food, drink as much water, or breathe as much oxygen as a large man.

Of course, the most fascinating question of all is, Could there be life on Mars? There definitely could be, although not animal life as we know it on Earth. There is no free-flowing water now on the surface of Mars, but there is evidence that there once was, and it is possible that there still is moisture trapped under the surface. Therefore, at one time there might have been a kind of life that could not exist today, and even now there might still be primitive life somewhere below the surface. Some life-forms on Earth can survive a long time under the harshest conditions: animal eggs hatch after many years, and seeds sprout after centuries. Perhaps such dormant life exists on Mars. Another possibility is that the rocks there contain fossils of extinct animals and plants. It would certainly be fascinating to see what life, if any, really is on Mars. I'd be willing to spend eighteen months of my life on a trip to find out.

And Mars is just the beginning, an obvious place to

start because it happens to be close at hand. Beyond Mars is a zone, or belt, of asteroids, and then the outer planets: Jupiter, the gas giant, the largest planet in our solar system, and its sixty-nine moons; Saturn, with its weird, complex rings; blue-green Uranus; Neptune and its huge moon Triton; and obscure Pluto, its orbit tilted at an angle different from all the rest.

Titan, one of Saturn's sixty-one moons, has an atmosphere about as dense as our own. We believe that Titan has a hot core and a surface of frozen liquids. If that is the case, beneath its surface ice Titan probably has oceans of various temperatures, including ones that nurture life deep in the Earth's oceans. Another destination is Enceladus, a moon of Saturn, also potentially having a liquid ocean. Who knows what surprises Titan or Enceladus might have in store for us?

Our entire solar system is an insignificantly small part of the universe, a grain of sand in an endless desert. Our Sun is but a tiny speck in our home galaxy, the Milky Way, which in turn is lost among countless other galaxies. With so many galaxies and therefore so many stars, it is inevitable that there are more planets than our minds can imagine. If we assume that nearly all of them, for one reason or another, are unfit for humans, we still have a number of habitable planets that is bigger than any number I was ever taught in school. Astronomers believe that there are at least 1,000,000,000,000 planets in the universe capable of supporting our kind of life.

If this is true, is it reasonable to suppose that our one little peanut of a planet (a character in one of Mark Twain's stories referred to it as The Wart) is the only one that has produced intelligent life? I don't think so. I think it's the height of conceit for us Wartians to decide that our planet is better than all the other 999,999,999,999. A more reasonable assumption might be that we are in the middle, which would make us stupid indeed, compared to life on some of the more advanced planets out there. A man who may have been the most intelligent Wartian who ever lived, Albert Einstein, developed a Theory of Relativity that says (among other things) that nothing can travel faster than the speed of light. If this theory is correct—and we have discovered no reason so far to doubt it—then visiting other planets with intelligent life won't be an easy thing to do. The nearest star, Alpha Centauri, is over four light-years away, meaning that it would take more than eight years to make a round trip, traveling the entire time at the speed of light, which is far beyond anything we know how to do yet. People wanting to visit more-distant solar systems would have to set out with the understanding that they would most certainly die en route, hoping that their descendants would someday reach their destination safely.

This may sound like an outlandish idea, but I really don't think it is. I believe that a lot of people, especially young people, would volunteer tomorrow for such a flight. A starship would have to be very large, and probably very comfortable. The crew would be huge, and you'd meet some very interesting people on board. After all, the Earth itself has been called a spaceship, and the only major difference between it and a starship is the fact that the Earth's passengers ride on the outside instead of the inside. Compensating for this possible disadvantage, and its smaller size, the starship would provide one important feature the Earth cannot: instead of being locked into a monotonous, 365-day orbit around the Sun, starship passengers would always find the view out their windows slightly different than anything anyone had ever seen before.

Will mankind do this? Will it decide to create Libra, go back to the Moon, live on Mars, visit Titan or Enceladus, venture beyond? I don't know. I only know that in my short lifetime, I have done things that would have been considered clearly impossible in the year of my birth. I expect the same thing will be true of coming generations (probably even more so), because the pace of human achievements seems to be quickening. Just think, it was only sixty-six years from the Wright brothers' first flight to Neil Armstrong's landing on the Moon.

I have dangled from a cord a hundred miles above this planet; I have been privileged to go beyond this planet's Moon, briefly, into the black void beyond. I hope and believe that some of you reading this book will be privileged to do that, and a lot more; in your lifetime, it is certainly possible. If you decide to travel, be like the kid in a small town, listening to the big diesels growl through at midnight, wanting to climb on board.